SMART GIRL

SMART GIRL

A First-Gen Origin Story

La'Tonya Rease Miles

Copyright © 2024 La'Tonya Rease Miles

All rights reserved.

ISBN-9798218566715

my tribe.
MEDIA

Book design: Gloria H. Rease

Author photo: Zoe Miles

CONTENTS

FIRST TO GO (WHAT MORE CAN I SAY?) i
INCHES vi
SPEAKER OF THE HOUSE 1
FANGIRL 14
TOP OF THE PYRAMID 25
REBEL GIRL 50
SO CLOSE 63
STUDENT MOBILITY 83
BASIC NEEDS 86
BILLBOARD (1988) 96
E185 114
NATIVE TONGUES 126
STUDY LONG 142
LONG DIVISION 147
ON PAPER 162
UNDOCUMENTED 183
TAKING CLASSES 186
CLOSE READING 192
I DON'T WANNA WAIT (PART ONEs) 217
I DON'T WANNA WAIT (PART TWOs) 234
DUCK MOUTH 245
LEGACY 257

DEDICATION

For Daisy Lee and Mary Elizabeth

"The very least you can do in your life is figure out what you hope for. And the most you can do is live inside that hope. Not admire it from a distance, but live right in it, under its roof."

—*Barbara Kingsolver*

"Art is chaos taking shape."

—*Pablo Picasso*

FIRST TO GO (WHAT MORE CAN I SAY?)

an introduction

I was in the third grade when my homeroom teacher, a tall, graying white woman, Mrs. Zajkowski, pulled me to the side one day.

"You," she whispered, "are going to college. You are smart and you are going to college."

I was a student at Lonnie B. Nelson Elementary School in Columbia, South Carolina, where I lived with my single mother who was a mere 17 years older than me. Mom moved there after she was stationed in the Army at Fort Jackson, and I followed some months later, departing my grandparents' home in Northern Virginia.

I'm not sure what prompted Mrs. Zajkowski to make such a declaration, which proved to be a prophecy. Mom was taking a few community college classes here and there. My grandmother cleaned houses and babysat kids for a living; my grandfather was a mail carrier. My mother's four siblings included two military veterans, a hustler/entrepreneur, and a convicted felon. My father and his seven siblings only completed high school.

Perhaps my teacher was referring to my advanced reading ability or my creativity. I was pretty shy back then, and I spent a lot of time crafting stories and creating educational games for my dolls and stuffed animals. I had an uncanny ability to memorize random facts; I was fascinated by the solar system; I knew all 50 states plus their capitals; I could read entire novels in one day's sitting. I suspect these are pre-college indicators for an 8-year-old.

Mrs. Zajkowski bent down a little so that she could look me in the eye. Most likely, I was looking down or slightly to the side so as not to appear rude.

I nodded and whispered back, "Okay."

I could tell from her tone and body language that this was a good thing and that I should be excited. But I was mortified. What and where was *college*? I knew of one older cousin, my mother's peer, who went but it was just like going to the grocery store. You go, and you come right back.

I thought about it for a minute, looked around the classroom at my best girlfriends in the class, Gloria and Thomasina—two other brown-skinned girls who lived near me, who liked the same music, who also liked to ride bikes and play dolls but who did not have 6s on their report cards like me—and then asked, "Can my friends come, too?"

It wasn't until I was nearly completed with my Ph.D. in English Literature at UCLA when Tracy Buenavista, now a total badass Filipinx scholar but then a graduate student working in my office, said to me, "LT, you know you are first-gen, right?"

At the time, I was the Director of the Ronald E. McNair Scholars Program, a federally funded initiative designed to prepare first-generation college, low-income, and under-represented students to earn doctorates and to become faculty. I, in fact, had been a McNair Scholar when I was an undergraduate, but I had not thought of myself as a first-generation student yet. That language was not as prevalent during the late 1980s and early 1990s when I was in college. Besides, I checked all three of these eligibility boxes, so it really didn't matter. I qualified regardless.

From that moment forward, after Tracy enlightened me, I had a term that explained what I had experienced as a determined but befuddled graduate student; brought into focus my travails through three different undergraduate institutions; and clarified my journey through nine different public schools from kindergarten through 12th grade, starting at Eastwood Heights in Texas. Once Tracy named this identity, so many things clicked into place for me. This is the story of how I came to know and embrace my identity as a Black first-generation college student.

I confess that I really did not want to write a memoir, mostly because it seemed pretentious, and my life does not feel very remarkable to me. But my daughter kept nagging me about it.

"Your life is like a movie," she would laugh but in a way that meant she was completely serious. "I think a lot of people would read a book about you."

After all, a girl like me, the daughter of a teenage single parent from a working-class background, is not expected to earn a doctorate, become a dean, or write books, much less go to college. But how does a smart Black girl get to college? This book aims to answer that question.

I am aware that I have played a significant role in shaping the field of first-generation studies and the higher education landscape, as well. I have established nationally recognized initiatives for first-generation college students at UCLA and Loyola Marymount University, while also offering guidance to other two and four-year institutions nationally. I have worked alongside high school guidance counselors and principals and helped them establish distinctive programs for prospective first-generation students and their families. I have developed courses that centralize the first-gen experience and influenced other curriculum, such as "Blacclimated" at UCLA aimed at supporting Black students of all backgrounds. I helped launch a journal about the first-gen experience and established the largest Facebook group dedicated to the population. I co-founded the Black First Gen Collective and launched a media advocacy organization devoted to the representation of first-gens in popular culture and mass media. And yet, I did not know I was "first-gen" for a long time.

The irony, of course, is that my foundational approach to supporting and mentoring first-generation college students and graduates throughout the academic pipeline stresses that *our stories matter*, that for too long institutions have ignored us or told us that we only count if we overcome extreme poverty and take our bootstraps to Harvard. Which brings me to this book that my daughter—and others—encouraged me to write. Time to walk the walk.

But being "first" doesn't mean only. In putting together my story, I also realize that while I was the first of the Reases and Websters to successfully complete college, I wasn't the first to attempt, and I definitely wasn't the first who was ready or willing to go. I uncovered a history of persistence among the Black women in my family and my community. In fact, my mother, grandmothers, aunts, and female cousins played a critical role in getting me to and through. This story is for them.

INCHES

a prologue

I could never tell where or when to place my foot. Too soon and I might tip over and possibly skin my knee. Too late and my left leg might drag from behind and pull me backwards. And what if—God forbid—I stepped in between? What would happen then? How was I supposed to take a step forward and grab the handrail at the same time? And if I didn't hold on to the rail, then what was I supposed to do with my hands? It was maddening.

So I would just stand at the landing, like a diver at the edge of a high platform, letting metal plate after metal plate go by afraid to move forward but knowing there was no turning back. At the base, those plates weren't even fully formed steps. They only promised to turn into steps, and I wasn't convinced that this promise was guaranteed. What if, when my turn came to onboard, the plate just stayed flat? I needed to know the exact spot to put my feet to avoid the world ending.

I stood at what felt like a ledge looming over a deep cliff with my feet and knees locked in place. If I was going to travel upwards then I felt like the plates were moving too quickly for me to come onboard; if I was headed down, then I panicked because the steps suddenly disappeared, and I just knew that I would get stuck and die. It didn't matter that groups of people gathered behind me with their large shopping bags, growing annoyed and impatient, only giving me a temporary pass because I was a child. They would huff and audibly sigh instead of straight up cursing me out.

My aunts would urge me and try to coax me to mount the moving staircase with them.

"C'mon baby," Aunt Maceo would say. "I'll hold your hand."

Panicked, I would look around the department store in search of some other way to get from one level to the next. My cousins, nearly all of them younger than me, would glide by on their way to our destination—either the children's section or the exit. It was just like the times we would pile into the family's milk chocolate brown station wagon and head north to the beach in Delaware or New Jersey. I hated the feeling of sand on my toes so I stayed behind on the blanket next to my aunties while the boys ran head first into the water and then turned and waved at me letting me know that I was missing out on the fun. I was unbothered. Safety was a fuzzy square blanket where I parked myself with a book – my feet safe and unharmed inside of a pair of white ruffled anklets that Mom insisted I wear to the beach.

In the department store, I wondered, *Why can't I just take the stairs?* They were fixed, and they didn't move. I knew exactly where to put my feet.

But this was the only path forward, and my options were limited. While squeezing my aunt's hand and holding my breath, I could close my eyes and hope that my red, white, and blue Stride Rite canvas sneaker with the white rubber across the toes would land in the correct spot. But that seemed too risky.

Most times, the only way forward was to jump with both feet.

SPEAKER OF THE HOUSE

For as long as I can remember, I knew that I was smart. My family, especially my aunts and uncles on both sides of the family, told me so at every opportunity. My mother's sister, Aunt Roberta, insists that I was a child genius and tells anyone who will listen that at the tender age of four, I learned and taught others how to play chess. I have no memory of this, so her argument and version of the truth stands. Aunt Rob herself was quite a whipper snapper having graduated from high school at age fifteen. But like most heathens and crazy people, that is, according to my Grandma, she moved to New York, which ruined any good sense she may have had.

My Aunt Maceo, my father's oldest sister, is more of a doer and led by example. Also known for being bookish, she started working for the Department of the Navy right out of high school. ("College wasn't ever on the table," she once told me.) For much of my childhood, my father was incarcerated, so I have few memories of him. Aunt Maceo was my primary connection to this side of the family. She spoke to me like I was a young adult and very patiently answered all of my questions whenever I visited my Nana's house on the weekend.

The Websters (my father's family) and the Reases (my mother's side) lived less than a mile from each other in Alexandria, Virginia, a suburb only eight miles south of Washington, DC. But there were significant cultural differences between the two. With my father's family, I spent my time working in a pack with all of my cousins—whether it was playing regular games of Husker-Du or creating our own version of The Jacksons, also known as Charlene and The Dyno-mites, an homage to Janet Jackson's run on the TV series "Good Times" and "Diff'rent Strokes." A lot of our activities focused on food, like baking gingerbread together and having large buffet style breakfasts in the dining room where the kids ate first and then headed straight for the basement to play some more.

The Rease clan, on the other hand, upholds independence, wit, and sharp thinking. Autonomy and self-reliance are highly valued. Knowledge of sports is a must. You have to be a quick storyteller in that family and never _ever_ back down from a fight, even if it's with your own relative. Stay on your toes and stay ready. If the Reases were a House, it would be Ravenclaw but in a Black Harry Potter universe.

Whether by force of habit or expectation, I would arrange my own transportation to see Nana, Aunt Maceo, and my gang of boy cousins who also descended upon the Webster household every weekend. When I was probably no more than 5 or 6 years old, on Friday afternoons, I would stand on a chair in Grandma Daisy's kitchen, call Yellow Cab, and ask for Uncle Shaw who was not a blood relative but a family friend.

"May I speak to Uncle Shaw, please?" I would breathe into the phone and barely contain my excitement.

"Where you going?" a gruff voice would ask on the other end of the telephone not at all bothered that a child was making this request.

I gave the address to the home my father hadn't seen in years and then would wait on the front porch for my ride to arrive. I yelled, "Bye, Grandma!" when Uncle Shaw pulled up in front of the house, gripping a few dollar bills that she left me as I raced down the painted over concrete porch steps eager to see Carlos, Kenny, Andy, and Kevin so that we could resume our version of "The Red Hand Gang," our favorite TV show.

My cousins and I took turns reading *Bedtime for Frances*, *Danny and the Dinosaur*, and the entire Amelia Bedelia series. But I was a voracious reader, and I quickly graduated to more advanced texts like Aunt Maceo's Stephen King collection, *Flowers in the Attic*, and *The Valley of Horses*. I didn't have any literary guardrails, and my imagination was allowed to roam free. No book was ever considered off-limits or inappropriate. If I could reach it on the shelf then I was permitted to read it.

Amongst this generation, I was known as the "smart one" and was the standard that my cousins—on both sides of the family—were compared to. It was common for Granddaddy, Grandma Daisy's husband, to point out my good grades to the rest of the family. Unlike the Rease boys, I was never yelled at for getting on his damn nerves. Everyone just accepted that I was a "bookworm" and a "teacher;" my greatest crime was reading a little too much and walking around with my nose stuck in a book.

Living up to this reputation as scholar in residence, my favorite pastime was playing school. Sometimes my pupils were my dolls and stuffed animals. I was just as likely to force Little Ronnie and Vershaun, my younger cousins on the Rease side, to pretend like they were in class. There was no greater joy for me than creating worksheets, grading papers, and customizing individual curriculum for them much to their dismay and horror. It was the weekend. Why did they have to pretend to be *in school*?

When left to my own devices, which was often as I am my mother's only child, I was content to snuggle up with a book. I taught myself how to read at age four and was several grades above reading level throughout school. I read at the dining room table, in the tub, in the car, and on the floor of Memco while Grandma Daisy shopped. Our agreement was that I would *stay in one spot* and read the latest *Little House on the Prairie* book while she shopped for various household items. I even memorized entire sections of *Blubber* by Judy Blume and sometimes recited passages out loud to pass the time.

My family viewed this behavior as odd but also special, more precious than annoying or off-putting. It wasn't that anyone else lacked brain power. It's just that I was anointed as Smart, which had implications far beyond getting good grades in school. My role was to explain, advise, mentor, translate, and report back. As the designated family ambassador, all questions regarding school and the government were first brought to me, especially in my mother's absence when she joined the military.

"Tee, you're smart. What does this word mean?"

"The school called today. What that teacher want?"

"Something came in the mail from the city. Can you open it up, baby?"

With Mom away in the Army, this role was reinforced when I lived with my maternal grandparents and a revolving door of relatives and adopted family members. I was front-facing and my main job was to help my grandmother who was young for a grandma but who was diagnosed with diabetes while in her thirties. I would read maps and road signs from the passenger seat during our regular four-hour car rides from Northern Virginia to eastern North Carolina where Grandma's family lived. I maneuvered the stick shift while she shifted the gears in her pale-yellow Mustang. It was my job to change the wall calendar in the kitchen each month and to make sure that all of Grandma's doctor's appointments were marked clearly in my best elementary school penmanship. I was the keeper of the S&H Green Stamps in the family and also the coupon clipper, which I guarded in the hopes that I would save just enough so that we would get a whole dollar off of Cheerios or Kellogg's Corn Flakes. These stamps, coupons, and collectible Campbell's Soup labels were like micro lottery tickets that I hoped would pay off and ease Grandma's financial burdens since Granddaddy wasted his money on liquor.

One fine first grade morning, Grandma told me that her sugar was "low," a common occurrence for a diabetic. She was out of breath and her hands were shaking. She stretched out on the living room couch as she tried to gather her thoughts and clear her head. Grandma was paid under the table to care for the kids of other Black working-class women in the city. Besides me and my Uncle Dale, who is ten years older than me and a teenager at the time, she didn't have any help with her young charges, one which had developmental challenges. If she got sick, the whole operation was on pause.

Mom was stationed at Fort Bliss, Texas during this time, but I knew the medical protocol.

I paused as I headed toward the front door, a certain sense of dread starting to pool at the bottom of my stomach. What if she asked me to *stay home from school*? The thought shook me to my six-year-old core.

"You'll be fiiiine, Grandma," I said, shifting my metal Disney lunchbox from one hand to the other. I grabbed a crayon and a piece of notebook paper.

"Here. If you need anything, just call the school. I'll be in Room 3. Miss Stein's class."

I grabbed the sugar bowl and a spoon, plopped them beside her on the two-foot-high coffee table next to the couch in case she needed to down a mouthful, and headed out the door to make the half mile pilgrimage to Maury Elementary School. School was my refuge, and there was nothing that could come between us, not even a sick grandmother. I <u>loved</u> school and would sometimes slip up and call my teacher, Miss Stein, a young white woman in her twenties, "Grandma."

It was determined pretty early on that I was gifted, especially when it came to reading and language arts. I was so advanced that I got to work with Miss Stein all by myself instead of being assigned a work group like my classmates. She came up with independent projects for me to do, my favorite being writing letters to Mom telling her about my first-grade life and all that she was missing back in Alexandria. I described adventures with my best friend, Leticia (also nicknamed "Tee," like me), and her siblings, as we ran throughout the neighborhood playing kickball right in the street. I recapped the latest episodes of "Good Times." I told her how badly I wanted Zips sneakers because they absolutely would make me run faster and jump higher. I added bright, colorful stickers all over the envelopes that contained my letters, and Miss Stein mailed them herself.

I doubt there was any talk of college at home, but it was clear that I was different—in a good way—and that I was going to make something of myself, according to my relatives and a few of my teachers. My family had decided that I was a prodigy before I even entered school because I was inquisitive, precocious, highly verbal, and well-read. Being placed in a gifted program and later Honors and AP courses just confirmed what my mother, grandparents, aunts, and uncles already knew to be true.

But being smart at school was different than being the family intellectual where I was supported and encouraged. Standing on the edge of Platform 9¾, I often found myself physically separated from my classmates or my circle of friends, leaving them to go to some better class or school or situation that challenged me. While I was happy to nerd out, I was also ambivalent about being away from my crew and sometimes my family—a dilemma that was only beginning in that first-grade classroom.

When I was in kindergarten, I stood out in another way. At this time, I lived with Mom in El Paso, Texas, and I attended Eastwood Heights Elementary. I was one of few Black kids in my class, and I regularly wore my hair in cornrows. Some white boys—I don't remember their names—teased me about this style, sneering that I had worms in my head. I was smarter than those dumb boys, and they knew it. But the name calling often made me turn inward, not wanting to draw attention to myself in class even when I knew the answers. I swallowed tears during lunchtime, my watery eyes steady on my Fat Albert and the Cosby Kids lunch box and nothing else. At times, I preferred a cloak of invisibility but my academic performance—typically high marks in elementary school— and the approval of adults would always set me apart from everyone.

I felt shy in school, and I did not actively seek attention, rather I preferred to stay away from the spotlight. But I stood out anyway. Regularly, I was the teacher's pet student and often was nudged to perform in some way whether it was in a school assembly or grade-wide spelling bee. Teachers and administrators regarded me as a model student, which seemed rare for Black pupils, it seemed. I was like a cyborg, someone to be studied and monitored.

Announcer: La'Tonya Rease, first-grader. A Black working-class girl raised by a single mother and her grandparents. Gentlemen, we can rebuild her. We have the technology.

I knew that I was different from my peers, including my cousins, somehow, but more importantly, I knew that I had a responsibility to do well in school not just for myself but for the whole family, my block, and even the race. This is what it meant to be *smart*. As the designated family representative, I was aware that I had opportunities that my mother, grandmother, aunties, and cousins did not. My success (or failure) was everyone's success and cause for widespread celebration. I felt the weight of that responsibility like a Girl Scout. I wanted to make my family proud and to support them the way that they had supported me.

Better, stronger, faster.

This recognition was evident as early as second grade. Grandma Daisy and Uncle Dale—still in high school at the time—

were excited when they found + out that my class was taking a field trip to the Alexandria City Hall and that we would have an opportunity to meet with the mayor. Our homework was to come up with a question that we would ask him.

On the surface, Maury Elementary School seemed egalitarian—students from all backgrounds and walks of life were in the same physical space, including the children of Congressmen who got to claim that they were of the people because they sent their children to public schools. But there was a clear racialized hierarchy already forming and subtle clues about who was bright and who wasn't. The Peters, Matts, and Megs of the school were separated from the Keishas, Beuforts, and Donnells within the same classroom— divided up by reading level and giftedness. And then there was me, in the same math group as white Peter, lover of some weird movie called *Star Wars*, but walking home to our predominantly Black and working-class neighborhood with Donnell whose prize possession was a pair of nunchucks. These divisions started early and lasted all the way through high school. Regularly, I traversed between worlds slipping from one reality to another like crossing a hidden threshold— where the rules, the language, and even the expectations of who I was supposed to be shifted with every step.

"Nah, Tee. All of those other kids are going to ask stupid questions," Unc rubbed his hands together after I explained the prompt. "You gotta come up with something *good*."

I was puzzled. "Like what?"

He and my grandmother looked at each other knowingly. "We'll help you," they said in unison. Uncle Dale pushed aside the mail, Grandma's various tchotchkes, and an array of toys that had piled up on the dining room table. There was always a bevy of kids running throughout our three story rowhouse. "The Brady Bunch" played in the background and provided the soundtrack to our planning meeting.

Helping me with school meant something very specific in my household. If it was just regular old homework—math problems and such—I was left alone. No one looked over anything unless I asked them to as it was a given that I knew what I was doing. But if an adult *volunteered* to help me then it was a different matter. This usually meant they had a point to prove or they needed to set a (white) teacher straight. For instance, Mom "helped" me when it came to a take home project about Egypt, making sure that all of the figures were brown-skinned and had broad noses and that they did not look like Elizabeth Taylor.

"White people are thieves," she told me matter-of-factly.

Knowing what was at stake, Dale and Grandma coached me in preparation for the momentous occasion. Finally, the big day came. Surely, I would've worn my best Buster Brown shoes, complete with knee socks, neat cornrows, and colorful barrettes that matched my blouse, as Mom did not play when it came to school clothes whether she was there or not. My classmates and I toured the grounds, fidgeted while the teachers attempted to explain the wonders of a democracy (a stolen concept, Mom had instructed me), and finally were shuffled into a small room that reminded me of a library. The mayor was patient and gracious, but I suspected he wasn't used to being around a bunch of seven-year-olds.

Sure enough, Unc was right: the questions were fairly lightweight.

"How many pets do you have?"

"What's your favorite color?"

"Do you like cake or pie?"

And then it was my turn. I stood up and held my wide-ruled notebook paper steady as I cleared my voice and read the question that Grandma and Uncle Dale coached me on.

"When are you going to pass a law in favor of rent control so that poor people can pay their rent?"

The room fell completely silent at first. Within seconds, one teacher rushed toward me and another headed toward Mayor Mann, shielding him from my audacity.

A classmate whispered to another. "What did she say?"

"I don't know."

It didn't matter that I had no idea what rent control was either, but I stood there politely while the mayor (now sweaty and turning pinker by the minute) stammered his way through a response. And it didn't make any difference that since 1950, the Code of Virginia has prohibited rent control and no mayor has the authority to overturn the law. What mattered most was that I asked the question. Uncle Dale and Grandma recognized that the average poor person or the average Black person would never get an opportunity to meet with a government official, so it was my responsibility to speak on behalf of others who could not be there. I understood that I was not to merely complete the task but to seize the moment when it was presented to me. Most importantly, my family prepared me and would take the heat for any consequences that occurred if a teacher thought I was being too sassy, for instance.

I was greeted with high fives and cheers when I came back home that day.

"What he say, Tee? What he say???" Uncle Dale was nearly shouting.

"I bet that white man started st-st-stuttering, huh?" Grandma laughed and laughed as she wrangled another one of her charges from hiding under the table.

I shrugged one shoulder, still wondering what "rent control" was, then I changed my clothes and ran outside to play having successfully completed the real assignment.

FANGIRL

"This check is going to bounce."

I walked alongside Mom as we took a Palmetto tree-lined trail toward the closest Kroger's. This was the same path I took to the 7-11 where I played Asteroids in the hot summertime and where I added to my Archie comics stash. One year prior when I walked this same road, I drew arrows in the fine whitish sand with a tree branch just in case I was abducted and someone needed to find me. After all, Atlanta is only a three-hour drive away from Columbia, and I feared that I would be among the child victims who were featured in *Ebony* and *Jet!* magazines, their faces all lined up in rows like a ghastly school yearbook.

On this evening, I stayed by my mother's side trying to picture what a rubber check looked like. Did it fit in her pocket? How did the cashier catch it? Did it just bounce and ... roll away?

At age 11, I was a veteran at moving with little notice. This time was a little different. Mom told me that we were leaving in the middle of the night heading back to Northern Virginia.

She was done with Fort Jackson and the military. I didn't know the particulars, only heard vague talk about racism (and probably sexism). Knowing that she wouldn't be transferred to another base (which was her request), Mom opted for an early leave instead. It had been her plan to be an Army lifer but at least she walked away with lifetime benefits.

Our townhouse was packed, and I had said my goodbyes. After the winter break, I would not return to E.L. Wright Middle School nor go on to Richland Northeast, the newish high school that was closer to our new neighborhood but nowhere near my best friend Pie and my other friends back in Charleswood. Allegedly, Northeast was "better" than Spring Valley High on the other side of town where we used to live. I would never find out.

In my brief one semester at middle school, I had finally gotten the swing of switching classes, which often meant that I had a lot of Black friends in non-academic classes like PE, but barely saw them again until lunchtime or after school. I had discovered a deep love of literature and history, allowing myself to be transported back in time when we studied ancient Greece and Egypt during social studies. Benjamin Franklin became my homeboy because he invented things and came up with cool sayings and didn't bother with being a president or senator. He was an Influencer without all of the responsibilities of leadership.

I also discovered young adult romances in the school library like *Mr. and Mrs. BoJo Jones*, and I was fascinated with a dark book called *Go Ask Alice* about a drug-addicted teenage runaway. The transcript that I would take to my new school back in Alexandria revealed straight As.

While I didn't quite understand what bouncing a check was, I got the gist. We didn't have much money. And knowing this, we were headed to the grocery store to get some essentials and to get the hell out of Dodge.

This particular Kroger's had a weird smell and I never liked to be in the store long. Instead, I preferred to head out to the mall that was connected to it, especially because there was a record store nearby. That year, Prince's eyes peered into my soul from the cover of his latest album, *Controversy*. I stared back. I wanted that album.

But this was a different shopping spree. Mom and I were on a covert mission that involved being discreet and getting lotion and toothpaste for the trip back to Virginia. Not on the list of must haves was Double Stuffed Oreos. I was obsessed with them. What could be better than the original cookie but with <u>more</u> icing on the inside? They were a full dollar more than the classic version: a straight up luxury treat.

I put my hand on the package as we walked down the aisle. I looked over at Mom with a shy smile.

"Can I????" I asked with one shoulder shrug.

I can only imagine what was going through my mother's head at the time. She had a nearly 12-year-old daughter to raise, and she wasn't yet 30 years old. The military, her path to a better life for both of us, hadn't panned out the way she expected. I had attended five different schools and was only in the 6th grade. This move would mean more disruption. And we were returning back to live with my grandparents, who had a dysfunctional abusive relationship as a result of my grandfather's violent alcoholic behavior.

We were leaving our home undetected and without notice.

She was writing a rubber check.

"Put them in the basket," she nodded.

And we got the hell out of Dodge.

My mom is an Aries, and I am a Cancer. These are both cardinal signs, which means that we are each self-starters and leaders. Aries are known not only for pushing themselves but also for pushing others to achieve their goals. I didn't know all of the details, but I was aware that Mom had put her dreams on hold when she realized at age 16 that she was pregnant with me. While I was snug in her belly, my father, who was four years older than Mom, had already moved on to another girlfriend and initially denied to a judge that I was his daughter. Not one to crack under pressure, Mom lifted her chin and told him that it was his loss. She never pursued him for child support after that, and he never gave any.

Not so much a coach, my mother was my ultimate cheerleader, urging me to Do more! Go big! Don't stop! If I had a germ of an idea, she would quickly think of ways to make it grow 10 times bigger often to my annoyance. I didn't hear "no" very much, but I did get a lot of "Figure it out."

We weren't always on the same page, though, as her short temper often flared. For a period of time, I used to wet the bed at night and would awaken—to my surprise—in a small puddle of warm pee. Mom determined that I was being lazy and believed that the best course of action to correct this behavior was to spank me with a belt. When I woke up one morning drenched in urine, I was directed to the bathroom where she awaited with my punishment.

"This isn't going to change anything, you know." I said, my voice shaky but fed up because I didn't see the correlation to the spanking and the bedwetting.

"What did you say???"

"Getting a spanking isn't going to stop me from wetting the bed," I told her matter-of-factly. "I just can't control my pee."

She never spanked me again.

As was true in other aspects of my life, Mom gave me space to develop my own musical tastes. The first album I recall laying claim to was a sleeper by my favorite Jackson, Jermaine. At the tender age of four, I turned our shared bedroom closet into a musical fort and listened to "So in Love" endlessly on my portable record player.

When I was five years old, Mom took me to an Ohio Players concert and literally put me on the stage during "Roller

Coaster." (I cried immediately). She would've been around 22 at the time and in her youthful prime. I recall bottles of TJ Swann being passed around our apartments, and I went to the club on base with Mom more than a few times. We were Gee and Tee, a matched set. She taught me how to play competitive Spades in case she ever needed a partner, meanwhile there was always some album playing in the background.

I have no idea what kinds of music other kids listened to, but Minnie Ripperton, The Emotions, and Rick James were like old friends.

And then there was Prince.

I think it's fair to say that back in the early 1980s, there were two kinds of people: Michael Jackson fans and Prince fans. I was a Prince diehard.

In my youthful mind, MJ was nice, sweet, and safe, and so I rejected him and his yellow sweater vest and soft jheri curl. Prince, on the other hand, better symbolized my teenage rebellion. Prior to *Purple Rain*, he was considered an outsider, a sexual deviant, and a "freak." People thought he was both gay and a sexual predator of women. Only weirdos listened to him.

By the time I got to junior high in the D.C. area, I was known as the Prince Girl, which gave me a bit of an edge despite my shyness. People didn't know what to make of me.

I first heard Prince music when Mom and I lived in South Carolina. She was transitioning out of Army life, and I believe that she had accomplished what she had set out to do: we had financial stability and Mom was a homeowner. Although we were away from all family members, we had each other and were thriving, at least from my naive perspective. In place of my various cousins and uncles, our house was filled with music—R&B and soul, in particular. Like many Black mothers, my mom often spent the weekends cleaning and would have Chaka Khan, Stevie Wonder, and Earth Wind & Fire blasting on constant rotation. One of my favorite things to do was to sit on the floor in front of our giant wooden hutch—all lemony fresh and Pledge smelling—and study album covers like they were research papers.

I proudly lay claim to being a Prince OG—the connection was immediate starting with his first single in 1978. Mom didn't bat an eyelash while I sang "Soft and Wet" and, years later, "Erotic City" at the top of my lungs, not knowing what the hell I was singing about. She could've easily banned him from my musical playlist.

One time she asked me to get off the couch and do some chores, and I told her with the most sincerity that I could not because I was busy visualizing the video for "17 Days," the B-side to "When Doves Cry." By this I meant I was imagining what that video *would* look like from start to finish. She chastised me, but I also got the sense that she was impressed with my creative process.

She also could've protested when I covered literally every wall in my bedroom with *Rolling Stone* and *Right On!* magazine covers. Or when I decided to put the infamous poster of Prince in the shower wearing only bikini briefs on the ceiling right above my bed.

This fangirl room decor started innocently with heartthrob Stoney Jackson and "Diff'rent Strokes"-era Janet Jackson. By 1982, I lived in an imaginary Minneapolis bubble surrounded by images of The Time, Sheila E., Vanity 6, and, of course, Prince in various stages of undress. Mom gave me the room to explore my musical tastes, and she didn't suppress my sexual curiosity or make me feel bad for having desires. But I don't think she knew that I kept a secret picture of Prince wearing only a bikini and leg warmers in a dresser drawer all by itself, and I would sneak a look at it before I went to bed at night.

The ultimate test of her parental patience and loyalty came in the form of a concert featuring the Big Three: Prince, The Time, and Vanity 6. I begggggged mom to take me. Instead of outright rejecting my request, she decided to play hardball.

"I'll take you to the Prince concert, if you win me tickets to see Chaka Khan," she bargained and then went out with a friend for the evening. She probably didn't give it another thought, knowing the odds were stacked against me.

By this time, we had been living with my grandparents in Alexandria for over a year since our return from South Carolina. I slept in the same bedroom my mom had when she was a teenager. When she was around 15, she decided to paint the walls a deep Chinese red, so thick it looked like paste than actual paint. You could sink a fingernail into the walls.

Frustrated, Grandma, a practical Capricorn, let the paint stay and it remained that way for at least two decades.

"Your mother was so bossy and *arrogant*," Grandma would shake her head in mock disgust as she recalled those days.

I used to hear stories about Mom being a loner when she was around my age. Apparently, she preferred to walk the streets of Alexandria alone, lost in her own thoughts, probably wondering how to break away and how to get to college, a place no one had ever gone to.

In response to Mom's double dare, I spent that night dialing WKYS radio like a crazy person.

Busy tone.

Busy tone.

And then the magical sound of a ringing phone.

DJ Candy Shannon answered and told me that I was right caller number 14. Mission: Accomplished.

Not only did Mom uphold her part of the bargain, I also was rewarded with a shopping spree which yielded a pair of black suspenders and a new Prince button to add to my collection. The concert tickets retailed for $12.00 each.

I found that my smarts, my intensity, and my drive could be put to very good use outside of the classroom. Around this time in seventh or eighth grade, I focused on winning a baby picture contest at school. Right outside of the main office was a bulletin board featuring black and white photos of various teachers in their youth. Whoever could correctly match the most photos with the correct instructor would win a golden ticket: a gift certificate to a local Kemp Mills record store. By this time, I owned every Prince album to date, including *Controversy*: the exception was *Dirty Mind*, the one I could not convince Mom to buy with her hard-earned money. But if I could come up with the $5.99 myself? No problem.

For two solid weeks I stayed after school, sat on the floor outside of that office, and studied every single photo with an intensity only reserved for Judy Blume novels. I compared photos from previous yearbooks and compared the likeness of every single picture. Once again, my research skills and tenacity were rewarded. I shattered that contest and went directly to Old Town with paper gift certificate in hand where I secured my forbidden treasure.

❄ ❄ ❄

The night of February 13th was bitter, cold, and snowy as Mom and I made our way to the D.C. Armory, which was basically a giant warehouse with some chairs. Prince was still regarded as an underground artist at the time and therefore it was not believed that he could headline a huge venue like the Capital Centre. There weren't even assigned seats in the space. It was all first come, first served.

Mom allowed me to run toward the stage during the first two performances, but I had to check in with her between acts.

"Stay where I can see you," she yelled from her seat.

I nodded that I heard her and scurried off.

Vanity 6 came out on stage in a full set of lingerie. Surrounded by adults of varying genders with teased hair and thick mascara, I stood there in the front row eyes wide open staring as Brenda Bennett licked a candy cane and threw it in the audience. I could catch glimpses of guitarist Jesse Johnson and the rest of The Time playing behind a curtain. By the time Prince and The Revolution started their set, the floor was packed, so I stayed with Mom back in the risers.

Prince stripped down and humped a bed during his performance of "Do Me, Baby." It was no place for a child. But what I lacked in direct adult supervision, I gained in confidence and navigational skills. That night, I roamed the armory like a champ and, from the floor, waved my arms in Mom's direction so that she could see that I was OK. In retrospect, I don't know what either of us was thinking.

A few years later, Mom was my Road Dawg when I begggged her to take me to see *Purple Rain* at a movie theater in Georgetown. This time she didn't play any games. She eagerly bought the tickets and did The Bird right along with me in the aisle.

TOP OF THE PYRAMID

My head was pounding, and I could barely see. Lately, I started getting migraine headaches like clockwork along with my menstrual period, and I didn't wish the pain on my worst enemy. There was no way that I could concentrate in class.

I raised my hand and requested permission to go to the nurse's office, all the way on the other side of the building. The teacher conceded and off I went in search of Tylenol and maybe a free pass home, although I really didn't like missing school and the threat of falling behind.

My head was so tender that I removed my glasses because I couldn't bear for the temples to touch my skin. My eyes were already sensitive to light and now everything was blurry and out of focus.

The hallway of George Washington Junior High—or G.W., as it was better known—was empty with nary a hall monitor in sight. There was an eerie calm without the usual hustle and bustle of 7th through 9th graders trying to play it cool and not seem too eager about anything. There weren't any boys banging out the latest Go-Go beats on the dingy metal lockers. And no girls singing the latest New Edition single or arguing about which member was the cutest—Ralph? Or Bobby? (I kept my crush on Mike Bivins to myself preferring to stay out of the debate)

I staggered and shuffled past the stairwells and lockers.

Pssssssst. Hey.

My shoulders tensed.

No one else was around, and it was obvious that the two boys behind me were trying to get my attention.

Hey, shortaaaaaay.

My morning just got infinitely worse.

I knew that the boys were watching my narrow behind, and I couldn't exactly ignore them because then I might be called a stuck-up bitch.

I held my breath and turned around to face them, scowling because the light coming from that direction was blinding and squinting because I couldn't see.

Ewwww. Turn back around! Turn around! They jeered and finally went to their destination, their cackles echoing in the hallway and in my head.

🏀 🏀 🏀

Classes were the least of my worries in the 7th grade. I managed to maintain strong grades while taking all of the Honors classes that the school offered. But I was still separated from most of my Black friends, including my neighbors who lived near my grandparents' home on Mount Vernon Avenue where Mom and I were staying until she could get on her feet and find us our own place.

Although I arrived back in Northern Virginia halfway through the school year in 6th grade, I managed to draw interest from the boys at Lyles Crouch Elementary School. I was a soft-spoken new girl with a slight Southern accent, a novelty act who temporarily broke up the academic year doldrums. Part of me wanted to blend in, put my head down, and just get through the semester. But it wasn't that easy. Besides my accent (I turned the lights "own" and not "oiyn"), my other distinguishing feature was my brain.

Lyles Crouch was a majority Black school. My Black classmates astutely observed that I was not in "regular" classes with them and wondered where I disappeared to for most of the day. After morning homeroom with Mr. Jacobson, off I went to advanced Language Arts and mathematics. Having these two classes alone shifted my entire schedule and kept me on a separate track from the kids I rode the school bus with.

"What reading book are you in?" someone asked me, eyebrows raised as they glanced at my red and gold patterned textbook, stacked on top of a spelling book <u>and</u> a Language Arts book.

"*Encore*," I answered softly.

"That's a seventh-grade book!" A small group gathered around me incredulously.

I was too embarrassed to tell them that we were nearly done with this book and would be starting *Accents*—the highest level—before the school year ended.

With my roller curled hair in a snatch back style fit for someone 30 years older, dark purple paisley blazer, and big brain, I earned the respect of my Black colleagues who, just like my cousins, came to see my academic successes as their own. They cheered for me when I was selected to read *The Negro Speaks of Rivers* during a school assembly for Black History Month. And everyone held their breath when I was one of a handful of Black students left to compete in the final rounds of the 6th grade spelling bee. When I didn't advance, I could feel the collective disappointment but also the awe and admiration, especially from the boys.

One of them in particular, a brawny kid named Moosey, laid claim to me.

"Your girl is smart," his smaller companion Beaufort poked him in the ribs. Moosey nodded, cracked his knuckles, and smiled revealing dimples.

In elementary school, the crowd parted, and I was nudged front and center, often reluctantly.

Junior high brought with it new rules and a re-ordering of who was considered "fly," cute, and desirable. The primary qualifiers were a fat butt and a pretty face. At age 12, I barely weighed 80 pounds, and I hid my body under nondescript short sleeve polo shirts and huge eyeglasses to correct my nearsightedness.

I was not exactly at the bottom of the G.W. food chain, but I felt invisible, which was mostly fine for me. Being in the spotlight was risky because it meant welcoming people to comment on your hair, your no-name-brand clothes, your off-brand sneakers. You might receive a red flag for not matching or for wearing *too many* colors. Being called a "Bama" was like a death sentence.

From the sidelines, I noticed the value placed on designer labels and recognizable jeans. The white kids in my Honors classes sported Swatch watches, shoved their sockless feet into brown leather Topsiders, and wore pastel-colored Izod Lacoste short sleeve polos with the collars turned up. But the kids around the way—mostly Black and a sprinkling of Puerto Ricans—had their own style. The flyest girls wore crew neck sweaters over button down Oxford shirts, sometimes an Oxford over a patterned turtleneck. Long sleeve blouses with skinny ribbon ties around high collars were all the rage. Nike Cortezes were a must have.

As is true for most young people, my junior high school days were filled with angst, longing, and a quest to be anywhere than where I was. In 6th grade I had started to become self-conscious about moving so much and always being the new girl in class and starting over. I had to learn the local slang quickly and figure out which fashion choices were in so as not to commit a faux pas. Silently, I cursed Mom for dragging me around so much. I just wanted to finish an entire school year in one place without having to uproot and say goodbye to my friends.

I spent a lot of 7th grade alone in my bedroom arranging and rearranging magazine cutouts of Prince, The Time, and Vanity 6 on the walls, and also choreographing routines to New Edition, Janet Jackson, and the Mary Jane Girls before the wide mirror on my hand me down dresser. My hips only swayed so far in my starched Jordache jeans, and my shoulders stayed close to my ears, but I practiced every night practically willing myself to find rhythm.

I obsessed over music countdowns and billboard charts, which gave order and meaning to my life. You never could tell when a favorite song would play on the radio, like the time I waited all afternoon to capture Andre Cymone's "Kelly's Eyes" on my tape recorder only for it to play the minute I went upstairs to the bathroom. (I cried.) A countdown allowed for some relative predictability, e.g., I knew that Culture Club would land *somewhere* in the top 10, so I could better estimate when I could go pee without missing "I'll Tumble 4 Ya."

Each Sunday I blocked two hours listening to Casey Kasem's Top 40 on the radio. Faithfully, while ironing my jeans for the week, I wrote the week's top pop songs in a spiral notebook dedicated to this project, eagerly anticipating who would knock boring songs like "Every Breath You Take" from the top perch and wondering why Casey never talked about George Clinton, The Gap Band, or Rick James. I did pick up random trivia concerning Madonna, Spandau Ballet, Wham!, and The Human League, and I preferred learning this information rather than the mechanics of prepositions that Dr. Gorski, my English teacher, drilled into my head. These musical nuggets helped me follow along with some of my classmates' conversations but mostly I ignored my white peers and their obsession with *The Hobbit* and *The Lord of The Rings*. Those books held little value on my block or in my home.

After school and on weekends, I would wander over to the Subway restaurant by my house to spend any quarters I could find mastering Centipede. My goal was total score domination, and I took great pride seeing my initials "LRR" listed in a vertical row as a Top Scorer. No girl could come close to that accomplishment, and few boys could either. It was a momentous day when Sarge, the manager of the 7-11 a few doors down from Subway, installed Pac-Man Plus into the store. I posted up there for hours and had my fill of chocolate Tastykakes and plain Utz potato chips. Grandma knew where to find me.

Bookish, athletic, deeply committed to the Dallas Cowboys and sports in general, I, a video gamer, was pretty far away from fly girl standards of the day.

My best friend, Shawn, and I spent a lot of time sitting on the front porch of my grandmother's home facing the wall of three-story row houses directly across from us, watching cars drive through. We could hear the trains rumble by shaking everything within a quarter of a mile constantly reminding us that there was life and adventure outside of Alexandria and G.W.

Shawn was a scrawny, light-skinned, and wavy-haired emerging beauty who was at least six inches taller than me, towering over many boys. Although we looked nothing alike, on Twin Day at school we wore blazers over long sleeve blouses with those trendy ribbon ties around the collar and told everyone that we were cousins. Shawn loved Michael Jackson and I still loved Prince, but we were a united front when it came to New Edition.

On those cold concrete steps, sometimes I would read a new book I picked up from the Queen Street library, which drove Shawn crazy until she reluctantly decided to read, too. Our favorite thing to do was walk into Old Town—headed toward the Potomac River—or hang out with the neighborhood guys, including my cousin William who was two years older and already at T.C. Williams High School. We needed those unsupervised outings to affirm our independence and to assure ourselves that we would not always be bottom feeders.

Doing homework was my least favorite chore and school felt like a necessary evil at the start of junior high. If high school felt distant, then college was light years away. I just knew that I was supposed to have good grades, get involved in extracurricular activities, and have a decent showing on the SAT. The notion of college felt like a murky means to an end, an unfun rite of passage that would help me obtain my ultimate goal: to be an associate editor for *Right On!* magazine and the right hand to editor-in-chief Cynthia Horner, my hero. Or a dee jay.

Despite my shyness, lurking within me, just beneath the surface was a spitfire who sometimes snapped. My classmates Tony and Chuck were on the receiving end of my wrath one day in English. I was fed up with them calling me "E.T." because of my bulky eyeglasses, so I flipped Tony's entire desk over—with him in it—and threw my copy of *Warriner's English Composition and Grammar* at his head for good measure. I was used to teasing from white guys like Chuck, but Tony was Black, and I was not putting up with disrespect from my own kind. I waited for Dr. Gorski to send me to the principal's office, but I think she was sick of Tony, as well. I got off with only a warning.

I was tense at home, too. Mom was spending more time with her friends over in D.C. going to basketball games and happy hours. A knock off for a young Gladys Knight, she was beautiful, single, and barely 30 years old. In her absence, Grandma was my interim supervisor. She would report to Mom whether or not I had washed the dishes as I was told or let her know if I spent too much time on the telephone. The schoolwork piled on, and it took me much longer to finish my assignments for English and life science than it had back in elementary school. The dinner dishes would often sit in the sink overnight.

"I know you don't have <u>this</u> much homework," my mother hissed.

I earned my first C grades ever in the 7th grade and was grounded. I was pissed constantly, first at Grandma for being a snitch and then at Mom for daring to discipline me when she was hardly around anymore. Regularly, I fantasized about living with my father's sisters over on Columbus Street. And I couldn't wait to get away from that hellish junior high school and on to my real adult life in New York or California.

I tried to stay out of the house as much as possible, and briefly, I found myself hanging out with the theater kids, nearly all white. I earned a spot in the school play, "Hey, Teach," where I played Tina, one of a three cheerleader entourage enamored with a basketball phenom named Jock Harden, of all things. As per the stage directions, my co-cheerleaders and I were to deliver every line in unison. We were treated as one character and had no distinguishing characteristics.

"Hi, Jock! Hey, Jock! Yaaaaay, Jock!" we chanted as we surrounded him on stage.

But in real life, at the top of the G.W. hierarchy—at least amongst the Black students—stood the cheerleaders, an elite group in a class amongst themselves. They epitomized being "fly"—the prettiest 13- and 14-year-old goddesses amongst the rest of us mere mortals.

Although it is not unusual for cheerleaders to represent the top girls in school, what was uncommon is who our cheerleaders were. In the mid-1980s, George Washington Junior High was about evenly split between Black and white students—with a sprinkling of Others (mostly Asian and Latino immigrants), but our cheerleading team was predominantly and unapologetically Black. And most of these young Black women lived in city projects or in working-class neighborhoods like mine. On the other hand, white girls, at least those of a certain socio-economic class, clustered in student government, crew, and the Yearbook Club.

Just like in *Essence* magazine, these young women reflected a spectrum of skin tones ranging from sand to umber to espresso. Some were thick and big-boned, others were petite and wiry like me. The cheerleaders were the It Girls at G.W.

The Blackness of cheer was evident not just in the members—the team also had a distinct style and culture. These differences were made clear whenever the team faced local rivals like Lake Braddock or Oakton in the Northern Virginia region whose cheer teams were almost always predominantly white with an occasional mixed-race girl. With their feathered hair, those girls would rally their teams with a combination of stiff-arm movements, tumbling, stunts, and chants delivered in unison. But to be a G.W. cheerleader, foremost, you needed to know how to dance, specifically the latest popular ones like the Wop, the Snake, and the Running Man. It was common for cheers to include lyrics from Chuck Brown and the Soul Searchers and Trouble Funk, local Go-Go bands.

Just like in a prison yard, every school clique had its own table during lunch period. The football players all sat together, and not too far away the cheerleaders convened. After grabbing a tray of tater tots with a rectangular slice of lukewarm cheese pizza, Shawn and I would scurry past these groups and head over to the interracial table of geeks, nerds, and randos. Our world.

Eager to improve her social standing, Shawn had her eye on making the cheerleading team that year, but I demurred.

"Come on, Tonya! We should try out," she pleaded during PE.

I thought about all of the cute girls on that squad. Belinda with her graceful athletic jumps, including the highest and widest spread eagle I had ever seen with my own eyes. Bonji with her dimples and bright smile. White girl Kim with her thick honey blonde hair. And especially Angie, the petite queen bee of 8th grade. Her dark chocolate skin glowed in her red cheerleader jacket. During games, sometimes her long, layered hair would fall into one eye.

I could not see myself among them.

"Nahhh," I said jarring myself back into reality. Maybe I should get involved in student government or something more academic, like the Yearbook Club. I was small enough to be a coxswain—maybe I should try crew. Did G.W. cheerleaders even go to college? They were known for being cute and good dancers, even athletes. But no one talked about the cheerleaders' academic prowess. Those successes were not made visible, which only reinforced the stereotype that cheerleaders are not smart.

But I wanted to be a good friend so I signed up for tryouts anyway, mostly as Shawn's emotional support.

Prior to this, my cheerleading experience was erratic and mostly of the guerilla variety. When I was in elementary school—no more than six years old—I decided that I wanted to cheer for Uncle Dale's summer basketball league in Alexandria. Although I never played on an organized team, and I couldn't run and dribble at the same time, I often think that basketball chose me. All of my uncles on the Rease side were ballers. Even Grandma played when she was a youth. The sport was in our blood.

My objective, even as a rising first grader, was to get close to the action, and I observed that those girls in short skirts on the sidelines had the best views of the games, so I begged Grandma to sign me up. I did not have a proper uniform—only a long-sleeved red blouse with tiny yellow flowers and a blue jean skirt. It looked like I was going to start gardening, but I didn't mind. Cheering was a means to an end. I don't think I learned a single routine; I just hopped up and down on the sidelines happy to see the game up close.

A few years later when I lived in South Carolina, cheering meant something very different to me. Pie, my closest friend at the time, and I spent hours perfecting our cheers in the street right in front of her house. We were unconcerned about supporting any team, especially one with boys. We Black girls—including Pie's younger nieces—cheered for ourselves and one another, chanting in our terry cloth shorts and stomping in our Keds until the sun went down.

And then there was the DCC.

The Dallas Cowboys Cheerleaders loomed large during this time. Starting at eight years old, I was enthralled with America's Sweethearts, the auxiliary unit to the Cowboys football team. Initially, I felt more akin to running back Tony Dorsett—another hero—but there was something captivating about a popular poster of five DCC staring directly into the camera with power poses and fog emanating from the floor. I was awestruck but never really saw myself *becoming* a cheerleader until Shawn raised the issue.

It was known that being a G.W. cheerleader would not turn you fully into a DCC but a lady nonetheless, much like *Pygmalion*. I had witnessed a few girls with rough edges make the team and become a swan practically overnight. And none of them wore glasses.

While I had managed to bring up my C grade as tryouts drew near, Shawn's report card took a dive. She did not have the grades necessary for tryouts, and suddenly, I was on my own.

For several days, we hopefuls trekked over to the gymnasium after school and sat cross-legged in neat rows adorned in our navy-blue gym uniforms with two white stripes on each sleeve. We were divided into small teams, each led by a current member of the squad who taught us cheers and gave us feedback on our jumps and splits. It seemed like every Black girl in 7th or 8th grade was there—with only a sprinkling of white girls, none of whom were in my classes.

I was unused to seeing the gym like this—more spacious and filled with girls who were less self-conscious without boys around. The squeaky sounds of sneakers filled the air. I tried to concentrate on learning the routines but couldn't help checking out the competition, wondering which cute girl would be picked, calculating my odds against them.

The last day was the actual tryout where each team would go with their leader and perform two cheers before a panel of judges. This panel included a teacher, as well as current and former cheerleaders. Among them was rising captain, Angie, whom I had admired only from afar, always too nervous to look at her directly. Our parents had run in the same circles back in the day when G.W. was a newly integrated high school and not yet a junior high. Here she was sitting at the rectangular judges' table with her legs, perfectly moisturized as though with cocoa butter, crossed at the ankle and not a hair on her head out of place. Her face was inscrutable as I nervously tried to remember the routine, to smile, to jump with my toes pointed and not flexed, and to maintain eye contact with the judges.

When the new squad was announced two days later, I wasn't surprised that my name was not on the roster. They included some of the more popular rising 8th and 9th grade girls that everyone predicted would make it. Of course. And so, I returned to my video games and watched MTV at my Uncle Larry's house whenever I could.

But no one was more surprised than me when I was pulled to the side about a month later and told that I would be an alternate member of the squad. This meant that I was allowed to practice and learn routines. After one week of that temporary status, I became a full-fledged member—finally earning a cherry red windbreaker with George Washington Jr. High Cheerleader emblazoned on the back in white letters.

The G.W. Prexies (short for "Presidents") were known for being one of the toughest junior high football teams in the Northern Virginia region. It was common for the team to have an undefeated season and many boys, including my cousin William, would go on to play for T.C. Williams High of *Remember the Titans* fame. I heard rumors that Mr. Boone, my salt and pepper-haired PE teacher, used to coach the team back in the day.

At the helm of this JV dynasty was head coach Randy Marsh. A tall and athletic white man who never ever removed his sunglasses—indoors or outdoors—and spoke with a drawl, Marsh was like our very own Eric Taylor. He wore the same outfit everyday: royal blue polyester pants, a white tee under a red windbreaker, and a cap with "GW" in white block letters. You did not want to cross this man.

We are not sure how or why but Coach Marsh also agreed to coach the cheerleaders beginning this year. Was it for the extra pay? The challenge? Unclear. But for the first 30 minutes of our practices—on the track during the fall and in the gym during winter—Coach would stand stock still with his arms folded and watch us perform a routine with absolutely no expression behind those amber sunglasses.

After giving some instructions with very few words mainly to our co-captains, Coach Marsh would turn on his heel and head over to the football field. The bulk of responsibility fell upon co-captains Angie and Nay-Nay who were charged with coming up with new cheers and routines and who disciplined us, as needed. They couldn't have been more than 14 years old. Marsh consulted with them and brought down the hammer if necessary but really collaborated with our leaders.

Since Coach Marsh wasn't in the business of demonstrating actual routines, information was passed down from captain to captain via an informal network. We relied on alumni (or "returners") who came all the way from T.C. to help during tryouts and practices. Sometimes they would visit during a football game and cheer the loudest in the stands right in front of us. They were our fans and hype squad, reminiscent of my days cheering in the streets with Pie back in South Carolina.

The summer after I made the team, the cheerleaders and football players were featured in a joint photo shoot. In our game day white sweaters and skirts, we pretended to play football on the field while the guys were on the sidelines. There are candid shots of us just hanging around on the field chatting with the boys. We took a group photo with the guys packed on the gym bleachers, while we cheerleaders sat in the front row. This picture appears in the yearbook under "Football" and the cheerleaders' names are listed as though we, too, are players.

Coach demanded that the players respect us and look out for us during and off-season, in and out of class. Marsh even tried to play matchmaker. "What about Ed? He's a fine young man," meant that he approved. But Coach frowned at the notion of any of us dating a "knucklehead," no matter if said knucklehead played football or not. We were a family.

I made the squad in the spring of 7th grade and spent the summer practicing in the hot sun to prepare for football season. At the start of eighth grade, I added new items to my wardrobe: shiny black and white Oxford shoes, crisp white ankle socks, white round toe Kinney Kapers, a two-piece white sweater and skirt set, and, of course, a red jacket. My hair now reached my shoulders, and I started wearing a fashionable mushroom bob instead of that matronly 'do.

"Why do you have makeup on?" Shawn would peer at me and squint her eyes. She had her hands full looking after her sisters, and we didn't see each other as much since I had either practice or a game after school.

My hand went to my lip.

"It's nothing," I said of the lip gloss. "It's just game day." A beat. "Do I look okay?"

I often stared at myself in the mirror. My face looked plain and unremarkable, and my body had no curves to speak of.

"No one wants a bone but a dog," Grandma was prone to say, and I was bony.

How did I get here? What did Coach and the captains see in me? It had to be my grades, I rationalized. Coach Marsh was adamant that I kept my grades up and regularly crowed in front of everyone when I was on the Honor Roll.

"Good job, Sleepy," he quipped like I was the dwarf that I was. He winked from behind those shades, arms folded as usual.

Above all, Coach expected team coordination <u>and</u> personality. Although our movements needed unity and precision, he appreciated unique quirks that each individual could bring to a cheer. "Style," is what he called it. That extra spark, shoulder movement, or rhythmic bounce. He abhorred laziness and was a stickler about splits, but he wasn't interested in robotic performances. We were openly praised for bringing something special to the choreography and not simply blending in.

Although we had a complete arsenal of cheers, the crowd favorites were the ones where each of us was called upon to leave our place in the lineup on the track and perform a signature move.

"Hey, Tonyuuuuh."

"Yeah?"

"We want to see you . . ."

"Do what?"

"Get down. Get down!"

This was my cue to ignite the crowd with a sassy body roll or hip swivel. But at the start of football season, I was terrified to move from my spot, much less get down in front of a crowd. I did not want to leave my place next to Keisha, a dark-skinned stunner with a megawatt smile who could easily pass for my mother's daughter and have all eyes on me. By drawing unnecessary attention to myself, I feared people would think that one of these things—me—was not like the others. Nervous to make eye contact with the crowd, I would conveniently leave my glasses at home during game day. I figured if I couldn't see the people, they couldn't see me, so concerned I was that they would scrunch up their faces in disgust or clock me for being a pretender.

But Angie was intolerant and non-plussed of my woe. She would regularly dream up new pyramid formations meant to showcase the strengths of the team. Being one of the two smallest members of the squad—petite and a little over five feet tall—I frequently was at the top of the pyramid. Or sometimes Angie would place me in front and center of a stunt to showcase my enviable straddle split. You couldn't miss me.

During practice Angie would take me by the elbow and guide me to a spot—often right in the middle. If I shrunk back, she would just look at me from head to toe and say firmly, "Did you think you were going to be a base?" End of discussion. If I was going to remain on this team, then I needed to accept all that came with it, including the spotlight.

The February of my 8th grade year, as I was approaching my one-year anniversary on the squad, the G.W. cheerleaders were the featured attraction at the annual George Washington Day parade. In 40-degree weather, we marched through Old Town with our pompoms dutifully on our hips, sometimes stopping to perform a short routine for the crowd. Younger girls and even some not so young stared at our jackets with envy—each of them looking for a bit of themselves in one of us.

Some girls like Angie were glamorous. Kim H. was athletic. Jill was the diva. I was the Smart One, but also the Little One, the Peppy One, and even the Goofy One. Sometimes during games, I would break out a move from the Charlie Brown Christmas special or mimic Michael Jackson's pelvic thrust from the "Billie Jean" video. All of those hours I spent mesmerized by MTV at my Uncle Larry's house were paying off. The crowd loved it and came to anticipate what silly thing I would do next.

"Why don't you sit with us?" Angie asked me with one eyebrow raised. Out of habit, during lunchtime I walked past the cheerleader table and continued to sit with Shawn and our quasi-nerdy 8th grade friends at the back of the cafeteria. Although my status went up, I maintained friendships with Shawn and all of my "regular" friends who were busy with their own interests like marching band or tennis.

Shawn was trying out for the squad for the next year—what would be our 9th grade—and had been like an adopted team member because she was my friend. She hung out with the cheerleaders in the hallways and after home games when she could go. But she wasn't a verified member so it would've been awkward for her to join the table, and I didn't want to abandon her. We had been through too much together and, after all,

Shawn was the one who encouraged me to try out in the first place.

I also was uncertain if I belonged at that table. While I was friendly with everyone on the squad, I wasn't particularly close to anyone. None of them were in my classes or walked home in my direction.

Why did the cheerleaders all sit together anyway, I wondered? That never seemed right to me. I felt like I was part of an exclusive club but I wasn't sure that I wanted to be part of it or that I had earned my place.

But I never said these things out loud. "I like it over here," is what I told Angie. So, I stayed at the rando table and would occasionally visit my cheer mates over on that side of the cafeteria and waved at all of the popular cute-boy athletes who became like big brothers to me.

"Corey likes you, Tonya!" Brian, Nay-Nay's boyfriend and one of the high-ranking 9th grade footballers, called out as I bounced by. I rolled my eyes and waved him off with a shy smile. Brian signed my yearbook that year.

As 9th grade approached, rumors started spreading about next year's co-captains on the squad. Like he had with Angie, Coach started confiding in me and asking my thoughts about the new team. Rumor had it that I would be tapped as a co-captain. And here I was, confidently leading my own band of nervous hopefuls through February tryouts, only one year after I joined the team. I had coached Shawn on the side, telling her to project her voice and to do a side kick so that the judges noticed her. I sat under the rectangular judges' table beaming. I was so proud when she followed in my footsteps becoming first an alternate and then an official member, just as I had and just as Angie had before me.

Earlier this year, I also gained my first boyfriend, Brian's friend, Corey, who was one grade ahead of me, popular, and also approved by Angie and Shawn. Although he was not a player, he was the manager of the boys' basketball team. We were both runts and the community, our circle of popular Black 8th and 9th graders, decided that we looked cute together, so that was enough for the relationship to move forward. Our union felt more like an arranged marriage at first. His status improved by dating a G.W. cheerleader, and I gained more street credibility—a win-win. Although Corey was headed to T.C. Williams for 10th grade, we agreed that we would make the distance work.

Shawn and I also had made plans: at last, we would be on the same squad, and I might be her co-captain. Maybe we would even cheer together at T.C. But only a few weeks into Shawn's tenure as a G.W. cheerleader, her mother made her return the uniform. She thought it looked "skanky" and whorish. During the summer between 8th and 9th grade year, Shawn's family moved 30 miles south to Woodbridge joining a critical mass of families leaving Alexandria for cheaper housing in Prince William County. Instead of G.W. for 9th grade and T.C. Williams for 10th, Shawn attended Garfield, a predominantly white high school in Woodbridge. The cheerleaders there were "corny," she told me, and she didn't bother trying out.

Meanwhile, I had moved in a different direction, as well. At the start of 8th grade, Mom had managed to purchase a three-story row house in upper Northwest Washington, D.C. thanks to her military benefits. The house faced Roosevelt High School notorious for being the home of The A Team, a local gang that allegedly listed its victims on the school walls. I continued to live with Grandma, Granddaddy, and Little Ronnie while Mom settled into the new place, and I settled in at G.W. I now wanted to stay at the school and to earn my place as co-captain of the squad.

As my 9th grade year approached, Mom decided that it made practical sense for me to go to school in D.C. She had done _her_ homework—asking around and looking up test scores—and identified the best public schools in the city for a smart Black student. Roosevelt was out of the question. Going forward, my school grades would actually count, and we needed to get serious about college. I needed a scholarship and, what's more, I was the child and she the adult, and I didn't dictate what we were going to do.

I sulked. I cried. I barricaded myself in my room. No amount of begging or bargaining worked. I was changing schools. Again.

Down.

        Down.

                Down.

I could feel myself falling back to the bottom.

REBEL GIRL

"What are you doing here, Miss Rease?"

Mr. Jointer sighed when he saw me walk through the doorway.

For probably the third time in as many weeks, I was back in the Associate Principal's office. Mr. Jointer, a Black man, oversaw campus discipline and worked with students who were "behavior problems."

"I can't stand that woman!"

I frowned and plopped myself in a chair that had become familiar to me.

"She acts like we're dumb. I'm not going back to that class. I'll just sit here every day," I said, not as a dare but as a statement of fact.

I wasn't returning to that class, and he couldn't make me.

American History was unbearable. Every single day, the teacher, a pale white woman with faded red hair, stood in front of the classroom mostly in one spot with a hand on her hip wearing what I was convinced to be the same fading blue shift dress. If she wasn't lecturing to us about the original 13 colonies then we had to complete worksheets and read silently.

This was "regular history," not Honors or advanced, the classes where students are assigned innovative take home projects meant to spur critical thinking skills. Somehow, I landed here, and I was livid.

First, I started rolling my eyes during class whenever the teacher spoke. Sometimes I raised my hand to answer what I thought to be an obvious question, and the teacher cringed and braced herself because she knew that my own bratty lecture was coming, starting with "*Obvioussssly* . . ." Sometimes I refused to speak at all when called upon because this content and its delivery were beneath me.

Eventually, things escalated, and she sent me out for disrupting the class. After that, I *volunteered* to leave and would walk slowly throughout the hallways to Mr. Jointer's office in the new auxiliary building, taking time for small talk with Shorty and Mr. Johnson—one of the hall monitors and her boss, the building supervisor.

"Girl, you know you're better than that!" they called out and shook their heads as I slowed my roll in lavender high-top Chucks, passing by all-white Honors classes, like World Civ, as I headed toward Mr. Jointer's office and the auto mechanics, carpentry, and air conditioning classes in the Career Wing that were all-Black.

This was T.C. Williams High School, the home of the Titans.

For all intents and purposes, my foray into D.C. public schools was a failed experiment. After leaving G.W. Junior High in Alexandria, I started 9th grade at Shaw Junior High, an all-Black public school in Washington, D.C. Located in the historic Shaw neighborhood and not far from the Howard Theatre and New Bethel Baptist Church, the school had an impeccable reputation and was led by a principal, Dr. Percy Ellis, who ruled for almost 30 years. There was a waitlist to enter Shaw, and students commuted from all over the city to enroll.

If you stood at one angle from the outside, Shaw looked like one massive wall of brick. But inside was an open classroom design that had become popular in the 1970s. There were no walls between classes and you could see and hear exactly what was going on in multiple directions. Some say the concept was meant to inspire student creativity and teacher collaboration. I thought it was meant to minimize trouble amongst Black and poor kids.

At Shaw, the students regularly spoke in unison when called upon. I was chastised for not robustly reciting the Pledge of Allegiance with everyone else, which Mom never ever made me say in school. ("It's all lies," she instructed.) Dr. Ellis roamed the hallways and often unexpectedly shouted into a megaphone at us. He was like a real-life Joe Clark from *Lean on Me*, the type of disciplinarian that white people can get behind because they are tough on their own kind.

There was a soft dress code at Shaw: no Timberland boots, untucked shirts, hair bows, or bandannas. According to Ellis, those things were signs of gang activity and the gateway to crime. Back at G.W., these were the signs of the coolest kids, including the cheerleaders and guys on the boys' basketball team.

I knew that I was supposed to feel lucky and grateful to have received a golden ticket to this school, which was an academic oasis in the city and also home to one of the most revered marching bands in D.C. But I was not used to this type of instruction or Black education. Despite the in-school racial segregation, at least creativity and self-expression were encouraged back at G.W. even at cheerleading practice. We didn't have to follow formulas or set curricula. But in D.C., where the majority of public-school students were Black, "tough love" was the order of the day. It felt too formal and also too invasive. There was no privacy and no room for individuality.

For the first week of school, I cried in the bathroom during lunch and barely spoke to anyone. I begged Mom to change schools. Even if I couldn't go back to G.W. in Alexandria, anywhere was better than this.

❀ ❀ ❀

Dunbar High School is exactly one mile away from Shaw.

Named in honor of poet Paul Laurence Dunbar, the school (originally "M Street School") was founded in 1870 and is the first public high school for Blacks in the country. Its graduates include a veritable list of Who's Who in Black History, including but certainly not limited to: Sterling Brown, Nannie Helen Burroughs, Charles Drew, Charles Hamilton Houston, and Benjamin O. Davis, Jr. Equally impressive are its historical faculty: Anna Julia Cooper, Kelly Miller, Mary Church Terrell, and Carter G. Woodson. In other words, the institution trained a critical mass of Black first-generation professionals who attended schools like Howard University and Oberlin College. The first three Black women who earned Ph.Ds. in the country either attended or taught at Dunbar High School. I would learn several years later that many of these over-educated members of the Black intelligentsia were denied professional teaching opportunities at other places due to racism and segregation and thus turned or returned to Dunbar to train the next generation. At the time, I just needed to escape Shaw, and Dunbar's new pre-engineering program seemed as promising as any.

Sometime in the 1970s, Dunbar High School moved from its original Tudor style building to a Brutalist structure. I had no idea at the time what the style was called. I just knew it was ugly. The school appeared to rise out of the ground like a giant slab of concrete in the city. It was difficult to see in or out of. It was also dimly lit inside. It's hard to imagine that a group of architects, educators, and politicians sat down and thought this was a good design for high school students.

Only a week or two into the school year, I left Shaw Junior High and transferred to Dunbar's experimental pre-engineering program as a 9th grader, a school within the school, which is intended to prepare "high potential" students into the fields of aviation, electrical engineering, and medicine. At the time there were only two cohorts of students, a class of 9th and 10th graders—sheltered and segmented into only four small areas of the school.

Like at Shaw, Dunbar also had an open floor plan and no walls separating classrooms. But the faculty tried hard to keep us apart from the student body at large.

"Do not mix with the general students!" Our pod of nerds was told repeatedly. "Do your work. Stay focused!"

We were college-bound.

They were not.

In a 1987 article written about the program in the *Washington Post*, Ms. Coffey, my social studies teacher, said that the pre-engineering students and the "regular" students are "like night and day."

In reality, our lives did overlap as we saw each other before and after school and often took the same public buses to campus and probably even lived in the same neighborhoods. We also took Spanish and PE classes with these students who looked like us but apparently were substantively different. While changing in the locker room, I couldn't help but admire a girl's crisp white Stan Smith Adidas. I wanted to ask her about them but remembered Ms. Coffey's voice in my head, so I stayed on my side. And during a school-wide assembly, where we were forced to integrate with the regulars, I sat a few rows behind a different girl who had an expertly assembled asymmetrical haircut. Her layers were perfect. I was in awe, but I never spoke to her.

As the late 1980s loomed, it was predicted that there would be more jobs related to engineering—that was the industry of the future. Secure and lucrative. As a result, I learned how to manipulate a T-square and how to code. No one asked what I actually liked to study or what career I wanted. It was just presumed that smart Black kids at this time should become engineers.

The problem started with *Romeo and Juliet*. I had already read the play back in junior high school, and now we had to spend an entire unit on it here at Dunbar.

Everyone dies at the end. I get it. I groaned to myself.

"I've already read this play." I told the English teacher after class. "Is there something else I can read?"

"This is what all 9th graders in this program are supposed to read."

"Yeah, but—" I stopped short because she was no longer paying attention.

I vented when I got home. One of Mom's greatest concerns was that I would fall behind my peers somehow and not be prepared for whatever happens at college. Repeating material I already learned was out of the question. That was the tipping point for her decision to transfer me out of Shaw Junior High.

Mom made an appointment and met with the teacher and explained to her the same thing that I already said but perhaps in more grown-up language. I already studied this material. I was reading *Song of Solomon* and *I Know Why the Caged Bird Sings* in my spare time. Isn't there <u>another</u> play that I can read?

The teacher blinked this time.

"She should not be reading those books," she said. "She is only in the 9th grade."

It seemed as though we had broken her brain. There was a 9th grade curriculum that needed to be followed. Mom and I were creating glitches in the system.

In the end, as per Mom's suggestion, I was to bring my own material to class and read to myself while everyone else discussed *Romeo and Juliet*. It was like first grade all over again, although this time my independent study felt like a punishment and not a reward. I bided my time that year before returning to Alexandria public schools for tenth grade and my ninth school since kindergarten.

At this point, at the start of high school, I was used to being accommodated for my smarts. Starting with Miss Stein in first grade, I had been told that I was special—gifted, in fact, and as such, I deserved to have assignments catered for me. I had learned and come to expect that teachers should be engaging. If not, or if the material was too easy, then I was given special projects to cure my boredom. Negotiating with teachers about what was best for me was par for the course.

When I lived in South Carolina, I was in "regular" classes most of the time with classmates of mixed abilities—although I was typically in an advanced math group with similarly skilled peers. The gifted and talented program in that school district required students to leave their home institution once a month or so and take a school bus to one of the high schools for enrichment, where we had a team of specialized teachers waiting. We learned how to create our own films and screened them for one another. We studied Purple Martins and created birdhouses made out of gourds. And then we learned marketing skills to help promote those gourds. We were gone for the entire day and were expected to keep up with all of our regular schoolwork. To be gifted meant that we had to have excellent time management skills, and it also meant that we had to be physically distant from everyone else.

When Mom and I relocated back to Northern Virginia in time for me to finish up 6th grade at Lyles Crouch Elementary, the principal, a Black woman with thick glasses, called my mother in to discuss my future. The principal carried on about my academic record and then offered a warning. I should stop socializing with Naquita, a Black girl in my homeroom class. Homeroom was the most democratic of all the classes, a place where different groups gathered in the morning before heading off to their different tracks, i.e.,

Phase 1-4—one being remedial and 4 being gifted. I saw Naquita at the start of the day, at lunch, and at classes like art or music that were considered to be less academic.

The problem, according to the principal, was that Naquita lived in the projects and was headed nowhere.

"Your daughter is too smart for that," she told Mom.

"I let my daughter choose her own friends," Mom said and gathered her purse ending the conversation.

By the time I got to junior high school, we were back to a school within a school situation. The phase four track evolved into Honors and AP courses that had more bearing on college preparation. Although there was a critical mass of Black students in the school, most of my classmates were white. I was reluctant to spend more time with them than was necessary because we increasingly had little in common. We didn't listen to the same music, didn't wear the same clothes, or have the same slang, and we didn't live in the same neighborhood. Although T.C. offered a fairly wide selection of advanced courses, including AP Calculus, I took AP classes in two subjects only, i.e., English and Government. I wanted to limit my exposure to all those annoying white kids after years of being on the periphery.

Back at G.W. Junior High, I started hanging out with Dani, Kim, and Megan, a trio of Black smart girls who had known each other since elementary school. Most of the time, we took the same classes and, just as important, lived near one another in similar neighborhoods. Although their parents were better educated than mine, the gap never felt wide between us, and I was welcomed into their homes like an additional daughter

But during our senior year, the three of them had different AP teachers than mine, so we had to make an effort to see each other in 12th grade. They had Ms. Buckbee again, and I had Mr. Welsh for AP English.

Patrick Welsh was a local celebrity author and expert on public high schools. He had written a popular book about the subject and even included me in a few *Washington Post* articles about racial disparities and the plight of suburban education. We had become close somewhat as he learned more about my young single mother and my absentee father while chatting with me after class.

The whole point of AP English I would come to learn is to prepare for the AP English exam. At the start of the academic year, Mr. Welsh had given us a list of poems and novels to study. As I scanned the handout, I noticed only three by non-white authors, i.e., Toni Morrison, Ralph Ellison, and Richard Wright. We spent the entire year writing draft essay after draft essay about Hemingway and Fitzgerald. In those mock situations, I was scoring pretty low receiving mostly 1s or an occasional 2.

The year prior, in Mr. Cannon's Honors English class for 11th graders, I had cracked the code. I never read *Moby Dick* beyond the first page but received a fat A+ on the exam because I repeated back what Mr. Cannon said in class and used terms like "megalomania" in my essay. He even drew a whale at the top of my paper to commemorate my accomplishment. But now I was stumped as I tried to figure out what was expected of me in this situation concerning reading that I didn't care about.

I had other things on my mind, as well. I quit the T.C. Williams varsity cheerleading team because I decided that the sport was anti-feminist and a white girl thing, especially after Angie, forever my captain, failed to make the varsity team and was regulated to JV for a season. In its place, I founded the Pep Squad, which was co-ed and predominantly Black. And although I was never a general body member, I ran for and was elected president of the Black Cultural Alliance club. That year, I protested the school yearbook, writing a strongly worded letter to Mr. Jointer and the head principal, Mr. Porter, about the number of images of Black student athletes versus those of white students as scholars in this year's publication.

"We do more than play sports," I wrote.

Fuck this, I thought. I don't want to write another essay on Faulkner's *Light in August*.

Without consulting my mother or Mrs. Barnwell, my guidance counselor, I decided that I wasn't taking the AP exam. Mr. Welsh insisted that it was good for me to take this test, which was an additional cost above the SAT. But I did not want to go back to Mom and ask her for more money to take a test I didn't want to take in the first place.

"You need this for college applications," Mr. Welsh insisted kindly.

"Not doing it," I said.

My answer was final.

SO CLOSE

The jingle of the telephone sounded far away, and my mind was in that hazy place where noise gets incorporated into your dream, and you can't separate reality from sleep.

It was the first week of summer break after tenth grade, and I was looking forward to sleeping in and catching up on "As the World Turns." I needed to find out what was happening with rich girl Lily Walsh and stable hand Holden Snyder since obviously they belonged together. Plus, I had a soft spot for the hardscrabble Snyder family, especially Seth who was torn between following his dreams of being a writer and taking care of the family farm.

But then I could hear Mom's voice from downstairs, and I was jolted awake.

I stirred, shook from under the covers, and shuffled down to the small kitchen, which doubled as my study space. The stove clock read 9:00 a.m., a truly ungodly hour. I picked up the wall phone thinking, *This better be important.*

"Hey, Tee." It was Rob from math class. "I wasn't sure if you heard?" He paused. "Len passed. Last night."

I froze, gripping the phone's handle.

"What are you talking about?"

Am I still sleeping? Is this a walking nightmare?

"He died. I'm so sorry. I know he was your boy."

To say that Leonard Kevin Bias was my favorite athlete—"my boy"—is an understatement. He was the star small forward for the University of Maryland Terrapins men's basketball team, but he felt like family. By this time, he had been named the ACC Player of the Year, the ACC Athlete of the Year, and was expected to have a highly successful career in the NBA. Lucky for me, Len was a local guy, raised and reared in Prince George's County Maryland, not too far from our Northwest D.C. home. It was exciting knowing that he was close by and that I could—in theory—bump into him anytime, like at the Hyattsville Mall.

One of the perks of his proximity was that I was able to catch many of Len's games on the local channels, and so I witnessed many of his signature dunks in real time. Amidst the collection of Prince photos on my bedroom wall, I reserved a place right next to my bed for a collage of Len. His smile often was the first thing I saw in the morning and the last thing I saw at night.

On June 17th, two days prior to this wake-up call, the Boston Celtics drafted Bias into the NBA. They were the reigning champions, had a 40-1 record of home games, and yet somehow managed to land the number two pick, which everyone agreed was an incredible stroke of luck and also downright unfair for the rest of the league. Boy Wonder would be joining a team in its prime and learning from the best, including Celtics greats Larry Bird, Robert Parrish, and Kevin McHale. The NBA's top team would get even better after snagging such a talent. Damn them.

Like the rest of my family and all Black people that I knew, I grew up actively despising the Boston Celtics. Despite the presence of Bill Russell (who I adored) and K.C. Jones—two well-regarded Black players—I thought of the Cs only as a white team in a white city. I wanted nothing to do with Ainge, McHale, and especially Bird, who, in my mind, was the whitest guy to suit up ever.

But leading up to the draft, facing the inevitable, I began to thaw. I looked deep into Len's eyes via the television screen and conceded that he seemed to be genuinely happy about the prospect of going to Bean Town to play for the villains.

Ok, I told myself and blew out a breath. *This is it. We are going to Boston.* I was fully prepared to join the Dark Side, and so I bought a kelly green snapback for the occasion and my new life as a Celtics fan. To have and to hold, for better, for worse, etc.

A few months prior, I visited the University of Maryland campus for the first time when my high school track team competed there. For tenth grade, I decided that I wanted to branch out from cheerleading and try something new. I had found my place among the sprinters and discovered that I was a strong competitor in the 200 dash specifically.

There was some down time between heats, and Coach Lawson said that we could wander around. I was on a mission to find my 6'8 soulmate.

All of the campus buildings looked the same to me: a series of red, brick three-stories with white columns. The building names didn't mean that much to me either: Tawes, Dorchester, Taliaferro. I was directed to one particular location not far from the track. As I jogged up, I could see members of the men's basketball team gathered just outside of the glass doors. This was fate.

I scanned the crowd. Players Terry Long, Tony Massenburg, Jeff Baxter, and Keith Gatlin were all present and accounted for. But no Len Bias. I marched right up to one of the guys.

"Where's Len?" I asked skipping past all formalities.

He grinned down at me clearly amused. "You're a fan, huh?"

I nodded impatiently and looked past his shoulder, hoping to catch a glance of Bias.

"He had to go to class. You just missed him, but he's coming back. Just wait around here."

Here was the Stamp Union, the student activity center and campus hub. I noted that students hung out here. The closest comparison I had was Rob's Place, the hamburger shop where Raj, Rerun, and Dwayne hung out afterschool on the show, "What's Happening?" It never occurred to me that I could go to school at this place. Or that Maryland was an actual college. I never saw any classrooms on this visit. No one from admissions addressed us. And the only students I spoke to were the basketball players who to me were local celebrities not people who studied or were earning degrees.

An elf among giants, I waited around as long as I could. I listened in on people's conversations, laughing when it was appropriate, not at all understanding any of the jokes related to school. But I had to head back to the track, my purpose for being on this campus. I gave a sad, slow wave to the players as I shoved off dragging my feet the whole way.

Later, over at Kehoe track, a teammate told me, "He came back! Len came back! We told him that you were looking for him."

My eyes watered at the realization of our star-crossed connection. I'd catch him next time, I thought.

Months later, on June 19th, Len Bias, age 22, would die of a cocaine-induced heart attack in a University of Maryland residence hall, two nights after being drafted into the NBA.

🏀 🏀 🏀

I actually had been to a few schools before I officially became a college student, including a stint at a cheerleading camp I attended the summer between seventh and eighth grade. Being on the high school track team also gave me an opportunity to be on campus but not once did I perceive myself as a prospective student. Before going to College Park, Maryland, we had a meet at the University of Virginia, the top academic destination for many of my white classmates. It was considered the place to go, especially if you were smart and serious about school.

From the T.C. Williams parking lot, it is pretty much a straight shot down Route 29 to Charlottesville. A mere 20 or 30 minutes from Alexandria, suddenly we were thrust into nothing but a highway surrounded by trees and eventually farmland. Home felt far away real quick. I listened to an entire LL Cool J tape the whole way down, occasionally making jokes with Rob, a long jumper, and looking out of the dirty bus window.

So, this was a college town. From my seat on the yellow school bus, all I could see were residential homes spread far apart, unlike the row houses on my grandparents' block or the one I lived in on 14th Street in D.C.

We had time to walk around and to take in the sights before our meet. I ambled over to the quad with a small group of friends, taking in the architecture and the pristine white buildings. People referred to the campus as "grounds." And then there was The Lawn. And the colonnades, the Rotunda, and the Pavilions. All I could see was: big plantation.

I hated it all.

I recoiled at every fact I learned about the place. It felt historic, yes, but not for me. I could not imagine singing "The Good Old Song"—UVA's unofficial school song—at the top of my lungs like Hoos do. If this is what college was like, then I started to have doubts about if I belonged. In my Honors classes, my classmates gushed over the campus, all of them excited to become a Cavalier in two years' time. It seemed like a rite of passage for certain students (The top one percent would opt for Ivies and saw UVA as a respectable backup).

Everything and everyone around me indicated that I should want this, too. I was told repeatedly by my peers, their parents, and my teachers that UVA was an ideal college campus. It was in-state and relatively low-cost. Applying there should be a no-brainer. What was wrong with me for not wanting it?

After taking the SAT during my junior year, I started receiving glossy brochures from colleges and universities in the mid-Atlantic and South that looked like UVA, most of whom I hadn't heard of unless they played in the NCAA men's basketball tournament. Bucknell, Agnes Scott, Lafayette College. I held on to the University of Alabama brochure the longest mostly because it had pictures of Black students, and I heard they had a good football team. All of these schools were expensive, white, and in uninteresting locations. How, exactly, were you supposed to choose?

Rob, who had become more than just my track buddy by this time, was struggling to figure out his own path to college during his senior year. His parents had secure, reliable jobs working for the federal government and driving the Alexandria city bus. They couldn't understand why he would pay good money to go to college when he could easily get a job at one of their locations. Rob was on his own to figure things out.

He filled out a pre-college form that the guidance counselors requested, including GPA and school activities. He also followed the recommended guidelines of choosing a variety of schools that ranged between "safe" and "reach," including the University of Maryland, George Mason, Old Dominion, and Wake Forest.

"I think you are aiming too high" is what his guidance counselor told him. "Why don't you look at Norfolk State and Virginia State?"—two open access HBCUs about 90 minutes south of Alexandria, he asked. Those schools were a better fit.

Rob was surprised and disappointed at this feedback. I was outraged.

"Forget that white man," I said. "Go see my guidance counselor."

Mrs. Barnwell was one of two Black guidance counselors at T.C. Williams and had become the de facto support system for nearly all Black students at the school who aspired to college. Counselor caseloads were determined by the first letter of our last names, and I was officially on her roster as a "R." But my friends, Dani "D," Kim "B," Megan "C," and Robert "M" weren't so lucky. They had other counselors—all of them white. One counselor told Megan, a future multi-generation college graduate, that UVA would be "too hard" for her. She also was redirected to apply to a "Black school," which presumably would be easier.

Mrs. Barnwell reviewed Rob's grades and extracurricular activities, which included track, football, basketball, Future Business Leaders of America, and working after school.

"I don't see a problem with any of these schools" was the edict. Ultimately, Rob was admitted to every school where he applied.

I approached college applications like I had approached nearly all school assignments, i.e., I took matters into my own hands. Mom was quite invested in my success and was at the ready to sign any documents I set on the table, including the FAFSA. It was like an unspoken agreement between us: I neatly wrote in her social security number and annual income as if this were just another form for school lunch or a field trip, and she signed approvingly and enthusiastically with few questions asked. It was just what I did, the kid becoming the guide, taking her through the fine print and dotted lines. This wouldn't be the last time.

There was no accessible internet, no quick Google search, and certainly no TikTok videos to make things easier. I heard about schools from my classmates, picked up information from college visits here and there, and relied on March Madness to identify prospective options.

Just as I had with Rob, I encouraged Dani, Kim, and Megan to bypass their assigned counselors and to meet with Mrs. Barnwell. During junior and senior year, we would regularly visit her office often popping in just to say hi during classes. She was the only guidance counselor that we trusted.

Periodically, the school hosted admissions reps from places like Virginia Tech and William & Mary who would set up in the guidance center or in the library. I don't recall going to any of these sessions, but I heard that these people brought lots of brochures and handed out branded tokens like cups and pencils.

For a period of time, I rode the school bus home with Megan so that I could go to the public library near her house, and then I took another city bus to my grandparents' house before eventually taking the Metro back to D.C. where I lived. Megan wanted to check out the latest *Young Miss* and *Seventeen* magazines as she scanned for news on Duran Duran. I was there for the college guides.

Among the *Fiske* and *Peterson's* books, I came across a new hardback about the Public Ivys— a guide to America's best colleges and universities, it proclaimed. There was something appealing about applying to not an actual Ivy League school but one that was pretty damn close. My grades were strong but not perfect, so I felt my admissions chances were higher at a really good public school. That felt more realistic, and I figured my family would still be proud of me. I didn't want to come across as too big for my britches either. A Public Ivy felt like a good compromise, and I believed that I was walking a tricky tightrope.

I scanned the list in the table of contents.

- **The University of Virginia** - *dismissed immediately. I wasn't going to waste anyone's time or money by applying there.*

- **The University of California system** - *intriguing because Angela Davis had walked the earth there, but California was too far away.*

- **The University of Michigan and The University of Texas at Austin** - *didn't seem that interesting.*

- **Miami University of Ohio** - *just sounded weird. Was it in Florida or Ohio? My family would be confused.*

- And no way was I going to leave Alexandria to end up at the **University of Vermont.**

And then . . . the **University of North Carolina at Chapel Hill.**

Chapel Hill is "perfect" and "the best college town in America" the author proclaimed. I calculated that this utopia was a four-hour drive from Alexandria but only a two-hour car ride to Williamston, near the Eastern shore, my grandparents' homeland where a significant number of our relatives still lived.

UNC was the perfect distance to my immediate family and my extended family.

If it wasn't a library book, I probably would've circled or highlighted the part that mentions that "Athletics are *really* important" at the school (98). Of course, I knew this already because the men's basketball team dominated the NCAA tournament and won a national championship in 1982.

A student interviewed for the book shared: "My daddy went here, and his daddy went here, and his daddy went here, plus a lot of other family in between" (88). I thought: here's an opportunity to start my own lineage, and perhaps my children and children's children might become Tar Heels someday. I hadn't thought through the implication of someone's great-grandfather not only attending college but *the same one that you attend.*

Aside from basketball and proximity to my family, I was intrigued that UNC was the first American state university, which suggested to me that it was socially progressive and perhaps even welcoming to Black students. That seemed better than an elitist, bourgie place like Harvard. I was choosing <u>public</u> elitism instead, the state's "intellectual mecca," the book said. I likely would've overlooked the part where someone said that "people just don't mix" at Carolina or that campus life was "somewhat segmented." In fact, Black students were banned from admissions until 1951 when a court decision forced the university's hand. The first Black undergrads were not admitted until 1955.

During senior year, Dani, Kim, Megan, and I met up in front of the school cafeteria for College Night where we had the opportunity to chat directly with college admissions representatives. The daughter of two HBCU alumni, Kim, a future engineer, was pretty focused on North Carolina A&T University but she was also interested in Georgia Tech and Virginia Tech. She kept her eye out for those schools. Megan had already drunk the UVA Kool Aid, so she left us early to join the throng of people who wanted to get on the Cavalier train.

That left Dani and me. Her parents also met at an HBCU, but Dani was keeping her options open. We roamed around trying not to make eye contact with any of the staff who were standing behind tables representing places we never heard of. And then out of the corner of my eye, at a table located just outside of the school cafeteria, I caught sight of the unmistakable Carolina blue.

My heart skipped a beat. I wasn't expecting UNC—*a Public Ivy*—to be here. With Dani by my side, I eased my way over to the table, enraptured by the table arrangements.

Most of my classmates skittered by, so I had the staffer all to myself. I felt like I knew something that other people didn't. I grasped the application booklet (yes, all on paper) with two hands, and when I thought no one was looking, I took a deep sniff. *This is what college smells like*, I thought. UNC soared up my list.

What gave me some pause is that the chances of getting into Carolina were pretty low for an out of stater. The college guide said that an applicant needed to have near perfect SAT scores or be a "superb athlete, musician, or actor." I did not have nor was I any of these things.

But UNC made sense. Back in March 1982, the same year that Mom and I relocated to Northern Virginia from South Carolina, my grandparents' row house was divided. Mom spent her time between the living room and her bedroom in the basement. Grandma retreated to her room upstairs. War was declared. It was the NCAA men's championship game, a much-hyped battle between the Georgetown Hoyas (Mom's team) and the UNC Tar Heels (Grandma's team).

In a strategic move, Mom recruited my five-year-old cousin Little Ronnie to her side. She taught him cheers and directed him to take the one or two flights up to the top floor to taunt her mother. Grandma was a die-hard Carolina fan and was sweet on James Worthy and a gangly Michael Jordan who few people heard of.

I was torn and felt like I didn't have a dog in the fight. I just wanted a good game. But I did create signs—Hoyas Rock! and Go Tar Heels!—for both sides, and I marched up and down the stairs with my homemade signs, poking Little Ronnie in the ribs for good measure when I passed him by.

The prospect of applying for and then actually attending UNC brought back those good memories, a time when three generations of my family exhibited school spirit—even if it was for two schools that none of us had ever seen. Little Ronnie would go on to work for the Georgetown University

Law School copy center for over 20 years, a job that allowed him to pay the college tuition for his own daughters, although he has yet to earn a degree.

By the time Mom and I moved to D.C., I was fully committed to the Georgetown Hoyas basketball team. I owned several Georgetown tees–most bought for $5 from a vendor on G Street–and wore a gray and navy-blue jogging suit–school colors–on special occasions. Ever the data nerd, I recorded player stats on loose leaf paper, and I studied the games faithfully while simultaneously doing homework often in a darkened room. Living in upper Northwest, with Rock Creek Park right at our backyard, we weren't too far away from the Georgetown neighborhood. We even bumped into my favorite point guard on the team, Michael Jackson, in the produce section of a grocery store there. But my primary exposure to the school was through televised games.

Some weekend nights, Mom and I would drive over to Wisconsin Avenue and grab ice cream cones while checking out the boutiques, as well as the pricey residences that kind of looked like where Grandma lived on Mount Vernon Avenue but cost thousands of dollars more. When I was bored, sometimes I caught the G2 bus to the Georgetown neighborhood on my own or with a friend. I first heard Madonna's "Like A Virgin" while walking past a boutique in the area. But I remained on the perimeter of the university, and I never went on the campus.

Yes, Georgetown was a private school and could be considered elite, but the winning basketball team made up for it. A fancy university with good sports couldn't be all bad, I rationalized. I couldn't think of a single Ivy League school that had won an NCAA tournament, much less made it to the Final Four.

My 12th grade AP English teacher, Mr. Welsh, also rallied behind Georgetown. Mr. Welsh had a brother who either worked at or attended Georgetown. He thought the school would be a good fit, and he offered to write a letter of recommendation and to speak to someone at the school about my application. What's more, he urged, Georgetown did not have any Black cheerleaders at the time, and I could potentially join the squad. What Mr. Welsh didn't know was that I had dismissed cheer because the sport no longer fit into my Black feminist world view. Instead, I established the Pep Squad that was open to all genders and didn't require tryouts.

Although the University of Maryland was close by and UVA should've been a no-brainer, ultimately, I applied and was admitted to Georgetown, UNC, and Oberlin College—the latter was recommended to me by a white classmate who would go on to be class salutatorian. Following my own intuition, I didn't adhere to the same formula of choosing safety vs. reach schools. Some people thought that I should have a longer list, but I couldn't think of other places where I wanted to be.

Always in my corner, Mrs. Barnwell supported my choices. When I received my first acceptance letter on Little Ronnie's birthday at the end of March–from Georgetown–in the mail at Grandma's house, I drove all the way back to T.C. Williams that day and gave Mrs. Barnwell a hug. Grandma kept the acceptance letter on the refrigerator for a long time.

❋ ❋ ❋

Mom went with me to visit Oberlin that spring. The campus looked just like it did in the glossy brochures that I started receiving in the mail—wide, manicured lawns and red-roofed buildings—but there wasn't much to the town. I remember being welcomed by a "Dean" at a luncheon, but I was unsure what job they had, although it sounded similar to a principal. I grasped to make connections to other places that I had been or other things that I had seen before.

I waited for the spirit of noted Black Oberlin alumnus and civil rights activist Mary Church Terrell, a former Latin teacher at Dunbar High School in the late 19th century, to take over my body and guide me. But it did not. At some point during the day's events, I made eye contact with Mom and communicated without speaking that this was not the place for me.

On the flipside, I didn't tell Mom much about my overnight visit to Georgetown. A yield event specific for Black students was still another two years away, and there definitely wasn't anything designated for students like me who were the first in their families to go to college. Instead, I came to campus with a generic cohort of other first-year students who were admitted as part of the graduating class of 1992. Most of them were white.

It was rainy and dark so the campus looked dreary and a bit sad. Georgetown students hustled to class and kept their heads down, navy blue backpacks thrown over one shoulder. The energy felt tense, not like the revelry I had seen within McDonough Arena during Big East basketball games. The day's agenda included sitting in on an English seminar where I pretended like I was interested and paying attention, but I didn't say a word.

And then there was lunch at the campus dining hall. From across the room, just a few tables over, I could see a handful of the men's basketball team sitting together and laughing. They were the only Black students I saw on campus my entire time. I wanted to sit with them so badly, but I stayed with my group and occasionally glanced over and wondered how desperate I looked.

That night I stayed with two white girls—a blonde and a brunette. By this time, I had a migraine headache, my energy was low, and I already was homesick. I told my hosts that I was fine just hanging out in the room and lied through my teeth that I was having a good time.

One of them propped herself on her twin bed and pulled out *The Washington Post*.

STUDENT MOBILITY

For my 17th birthday, Mom surprised me with a sparkly metallic gray 1974 Volkswagen beetle that I named Kirby. She dropped it off while I was attending a residential academic enrichment program at George Mason University during the summer between my junior and senior year of high school.

This was a controversial decision, an audible that I called, without consulting her. I had been admitted to a prestigious summer program hosted by the city of Alexandria for advanced students interested in economics, and I would receive a stipend for my work. Hoping for a more authentic precollege experience and suspicious that I would hate economics, I instead submitted paperwork to attend the GMU honors program where I got to take a real college class, and Mom had to pay for it.

I didn't know how to maneuver a stick shift yet but somehow had to drive that car around the Beltway back home.

"Figure it out," Mom said before she hopped in her friend's vehicle and drove off.

I should've expected this pronouncement. As usual, most of Mom's gifts came in the form of sage and unwanted advice.

There was a practical reason for this particular reward. We had moved again. This time, Mom had purchased a split-level brick home in Southern Maryland. With only one year of school left, it didn't make any sense for me to transfer schools, so every morning, Kirby and I crossed the Woodrow Wilson Bridge which connected Southern Maryland to Northern Virginia. But the traffic was finicky and unpredictable, and no matter how early I left home, I was regularly late to first period, French 3.

Madame Adams did not tolerate tardiness, and she scolded me every time I walked in sheepishly.

"Chantal!" she would admonish me, using my chosen French name.

I made up every excuse I could think of because I could not tell her that I did not in fact live in Alexandria but in a different state altogether: I wasn't feeling well. My grandma was sick. I didn't hear my alarm. If I arrived too far beyond the hour, sometimes I would just sit in the car, listen to WKYS on the radio, and wait out first period. Better never to class than late.

Not since 7th grade had I attended my neighborhood school or given my correct home address to school authorities. When I lived in D.C. during tenth and eleventh grades, I had to: wake up every day by 5:00 a.m. and leave no later than 5:17 a.m. sharp; catch the #52, 53, or 54 bus three miles down 14th Street to the McPherson Square Metrorail station; take a 33 minute ride past the Smithsonian, the Pentagon, and National Airport to the Braddock Road stop in Alexandria; and walk to an official T.C. Williams school bus stop nearby, pretending like I had just come from my grandmother's house around the corner, and catch a yellow bus to school all before 7:20 a.m.

Never give away your real address. That was the drill.

Mme Adams gave me the stink eye, scolded me en Francais, and assigned me indefinite afterschool detention for the whole year. I was a good and smart student, so she couldn't understand my perpetual tardiness.

"Que se passe-t-il?" she asked. What is going on?

But I couldn't break.

"Je suis désolée," I said.

"Je suis vraiment désolée," I pleaded.

Snitches get stitches, I knew.

BASIC NEEDS

One of my favorite t-shirts that I wore growing up once belonged to my older cousin, Lenita, who is 12 years my senior. It was a distressed grey short sleeve that had *Elizabeth City State University* emblazoned across the chest. I had never been to the school—barely knew where Elizabeth City was—but I felt quite smart when I wore it.

For a long time, Neet was the only person in the family I knew who had gone to college—outside of another relative who had taken night classes and earned a degree after she was married and had a baby. I figured that by wearing Lenita's castaway shirt, I would absorb her good fortune and I would be one step closer to accomplishing the same feat.

Lenita was raised in a white, one-story weather-beaten family home that Grandma Daisy purchased for her parents in Williamston, North Carolina, a small town of about 5,500 residents in Eastern Carolina, not too far from Greenville and about an hour south of Elizabeth City. I recall there being two primary landmarks in the town when I would come to visit my great aunts and great uncles during the summer as a child: a Wonder Bread bakery directly across the street from The House, as we affectionately called it, and a Holiday Inn a little bit farther down the road.

To pass the time when she was a child, Neet, our cousins, and her friends would ride bikes and roller skate in the dip where bakery products were unloaded. Back in the day, you could buy a loaf of bread for just 25 cents. With only ten cents, you could get hand-sized cakes and still have change left over. Neet's favorite was called the banana split, which was like a taco but made out of cake with lemon cream inside. Weighing barely 100 pounds, she could eat two or three at once and often did.

Back then, the smell of freshly baked bread filled the air. Nowadays, Williamston is the type of place where so-called "deaths of despair" proliferate—where drug overdoses, suicides, and liver disease account for a growing number of deaths among younger and younger Americans, especially among the poor, white, and rural. In 2023, Martin General, the local hospital, filed for bankruptcy and closed its doors. That same year, a months-long investigation led to the arrest of 25 people in the local area wanted for various crimes ranging from possession of to intent to distribute cocaine, heroin, or meth. The Wonder Bread building is still there but it sits empty.

Only a handful of Grandma's twelve siblings left their hometown and moved to bigger Northern cities like Washington, D.C., New York, and Stamford. Aunt Nettie, a middle child, stayed in Williamston to care for their parents, my great-grandmother, Annie Bruce and my great-grandfather,

Edward Rease. She had no biological children of her own but welcomed the granddaughter of her eldest sister, my great aunt Phoebe. That baby girl was Lenita.

In that weather beaten house lived Lenita, Aunt Nettie, and her younger brother, my great uncle Dick, and his four children: Agnes, Brian, Craig, and Richard. Uncle Dick was a bricklayer who only worked in the summer months. When the weather turned cold, there was no work, and the seven of them depended upon the $35 Aunt Nettie made every week working as a maid for the mayor and his daughter.

Mayor Green made sure that the family had oil in the winter. And in the summer, the kids helped Aunt Nettie and Uncle Dick with canning corn, lima beans, string beans, and beets to prepare for those colder months. Despite not having much, Neet never felt poor or like she lacked for anything.

According to Lenita there were four kinds of Black people in Williamston: those who were bad off, those who were *really* bad off, those who weren't as bad off, and those who had a little something. Our family wasn't as bad off. Although money might get tight, there was enough to go around and nobody ever went hungry.

Light-skinned families always did better, Neet observed. College-educated and fair-complexioned, the Boones were part of the Williamston Black upper echelon. In 1961, Rocky Mount native son Herman Boone relocated to the area and became the head football coach of E.J. Hayes High School, amassing a 99-8 record over nine years.

From first through eighth grade, Lenita attended Hayes, then an all-Black school, formerly known as the Williamston Colored School. The teachers were caring but also tough. If you got out of line, you might get paddled at school and then receive a spanking when you got home, too. School desegregation took its time getting to Williamston, arriving slowly and in waves. First, the white teachers appeared at Hayes testing the waters. And then came the white students. Eventually, Lenita would go to high school across town in a white neighborhood and was among the first class to graduate from that newly integrated school in 1975.

After the schools were forced to desegregate, Boone was offered an assistant coach position because, according to the school board, the town was "not ready for a Black coach"—despite his honey-colored skin and winning record. He declined and took a job as a PE teacher and assistant football coach at T.C. Williams High School in Alexandria, Virginia, where he would establish another legacy with the famed Titans.

As Lenita approached the end of her high school career, she had a big decision ahead of her. She desperately wanted to get a good job and to make her mother proud. But a good job for a brown-skinned girl living in the country was hard to come by. Mayor Green's daughter offered her a job in janitorial services, but Neet was too smart for that. Her prior working experience included picking tobacco in the hot sun, leaving her hands stained and dirty. She never wanted to do that again.

But her greatest fear was ending up young, married, barefoot, and pregnant, chasing after some pot-bellied man with a trail of screaming children behind her. She shuddered at the thought and imagined a scenario where she was not in Williamston but someplace more exciting like Alexandria, Virginia where Coach Boone relocated and where her big cousin, my mother, lived.

Neet is about five years younger than my mother and briefly, their time together overlapped in Williamston, where Mom was born. Eventually, Mom joined Grandma and her husband—the man I would know as my grandfather—in their new home in Alexandria, leaving Neet behind. Neet would spend the summer in Alexandria hanging out with her older cousins. She had French toast for the first time up there.

You need to get away from that little town, my mother would tell her.

By this time, Mom, who was a teenaged single parent, had fallen from grace. Meeting everyone's low expectations, her life was now a cautionary tale, an example of what Lenita ought not to do.

College became the way out. Only problem was no other Rease had ever gone, not even attempted. Hell, most Black people in Williamston didn't want to go to school and didn't see the point. It simply wasn't the norm. White kids, on the other hand, went to college or worked in a family business or both.

Coach Boone, a two-time graduate of North Carolina Central University, had encouraged the local Williamston kids to go to school. But he primarily focused on the boys, reminding them that playing football could be a pathway to college. He and his family had moved to Alexandria years before Neet was ready to apply. She tried her best to recall the advice that he passed down while she was hanging out with his daughter, Sharron.

With little guidance but a lot of optimism, Lenita applied to a number of schools in state—sight unseen—all of them HBCUs, including Johnson C. Smith in Charlotte. Although the school is less than 30 miles away from Williamston, Neet didn't give a single thought to East Carolina University over in Greenville. ECU had only begun admitting Black students about a decade earlier in 1962, and the first Black faculty arrived in 1974 when Lenita was in high school. HBCUs were the only schools she considered or even seemed welcoming. She decided that North Carolina A&T was too far away and ultimately chose Elizabeth City because it was close to home and relatively affordable, plus she actually knew people who went there, like her neighbor Marvin and local star athlete, Aly Khan Johnson.

Founded in 1891 by Hugh Cale, a Black representative in the N.C. General Assembly, Elizabeth City is one of the smallest public institutions in the state. According to its website, the school is "uniquely located in a geographic region with a population that is primarily characterized as both low-income and rural. Often students from this region are first-generation college students." As of fall 2023, the tuition is $500/semester.

Aunt Nettie and Uncle Dick were very proud.

From Lenita's perspective, Elizabeth City was in fact a big city. She roomed with two friends from Williamston in Bias Hall named after Dr. John Henry Bias, the school's second president. Elizabeth City has only had Black leaders at the helm, including two women, i.e., Dr. Stacey Franklin Jones and Dr. Karrie G. Dixon.

Neet immediately realized some of the perks of going to college that had nothing to do with getting a degree or a good job. For instance, no curfew. She could stay out *as late as 11:30 p.m.* and not have to worry about a tongue lashing from Aunt Nettie. She also heard Spanish for the first time—thought that the whole world spoke English before that. It was a good thing that her professor was sympathetic, too, because she did not truly earn that "B" grade she received in the class.

But you couldn't put a grade or a price on freedom. Lenita met Black people from so many different places, including folks who were from the D.C. area, many of whom knew her cousins in Alexandria. They were like older siblings who looked out for her, especially since she was a wide-eyed freshman who was good for the picking. She had fun, she met boys, and she didn't call home too much because that was a collect call.

Lenita's biggest challenge wasn't the schoolwork or even the distance. It was her growling belly. The school cafeteria shut down at 6:00 p.m. every night, leaving the student body to fend for themselves. If you had a refrigerator or a coveted microwave in your room, you could get by. Lenita had neither. In fact, she wished she even had Cup Of Noodles, something to fill her up, but that would've been considered a delicacy.

Aunt Nettie rarely sent anything, couldn't really. Sometimes when Marvin came to Williamston for a visit, she slipped him $10 to take back to Lenita. Neet desperately tried to eat as much as she could in the dining hall but not being much of a binger, she filled up quickly. By 10:00 a.m. she was starving all over again, trying to concentrate on classes. No wonder her grades weren't strong.

To pass the time and to keep her mind off her worries, Lenita danced. To the tunes of the Ohio Players, Cameo, Brick, and Earth Wind & Fire, Lenita and her roommates did The Bump and The Bus Stop. Some of these dances she picked up from her visits up North and brought them back to campus, which increased her popularity. Not to mention, usually there were chips or some other food at these dance parties.

All of that dancing caught the eye of sorority members who were always on the lookout for talented students to add to their roster. During sophomore year, Neet used $130 of her summer savings working in Alexandria to participate in the pledge process. It was a grueling months long endeavor that involved late nights spent reciting historical facts and pleasing but most often—displeasing—Big Sisters. That part she expected. The not eating part is what sent her over the edge. The pledges were restricted to a diet of onions and you could *never* be caught eating in public or risk being paddled late at night during set.

By Hell Week, Lenita was malnourished, as well as physically and mentally drained. Her mind whirled with sorority facts and dates and line names in addition to her own schoolwork. One night during a meeting while Lenita and her fellow pledges stood for hours while being pestered with questions, a Big Sister slapped Neet in the face *hard*. Before coming to college, she had been paddled before, but not like this. She had been tired before, but not like this. And never in her life had she been this hungry.

Lenita didn't think. She only reacted, a decision that was costly and irreversible. After Neet struck back, she received a beat down that night and was dropped from line—seven days before she would have crossed and become an official member.

Lenita completed 56 credit hours by the time she decided not to return to Elizabeth City. She was not a member of the illustrious sorority and had nothing to show but bad grades. The last thing she wanted to do was go back home and be one more mouth to feed, not when so many people knew that she had gone off to college. And she absolutely could not make her mother—and the family—look bad.

While she was chasing some guy up in Cincinnati facing the coldest weather imaginable, the wind literally blew her into an Army recruitment center. The recruiter promised a steady income and three squares a day. She was sold.

"I left school because I was hungry," she told me decades later, long after I donated the shirt to Goodwill.

When she gifted me that old grey ECSU t-shirt, I didn't know that Lenita hadn't graduated from the school. In my mind, that piece of clothing was evidence of success and was enough to propel me to follow in her footsteps. Now I had to run my own race. Lenita took things as far as she could go and passed the baton to me.

BILLBOARD (1988)

"CussWords," Too Short
uncharted

During my junior year in high school, I started working after school at a dog grooming store about a half mile away from T.C. Williams, near the Fairlington neighborhood on the westside of Alexandria. I found out about the job from Wendy, a fellow member of the JV cheerleading team. The JV squad actually was not my intended destination. Having cheered at G.W. Junior High and nearly being co-captain, I tried out for the varsity team full of confidence and pep. I convinced my friend Kimberly, a tall, wavy-haired, and completely uncoordinated white girl to try out, as well. Unlike at G.W., being a good dancer wasn't a requirement for TCW cheerleading, and Kim was a looker. Also, unlike at G.W., there were more white girls on the squad. Kim and I practiced together after school, and I tried my best to teach her the Cabbage Patch, but she was hopeless. Just like in a script from a castaway John Hughes movie, Kim made the team, and I did not.

I had a brief stint as JV captain and a regular member of the varsity squad, but I eventually abandoned the entire cheerleading enterprise by 11th grade. I needed paid opportunities to develop my resume, anyway.

To start, Wendy and I answered the telephone, made reservations, and put shipment away at the grooming shop. Over time, we graduated to bathing the dogs with Joy dishwashing liquid before handing them over to the experienced groomers. Most of the clientele were middle-aged or older white people who lived close by and who brought in their Yorkis, Lhasa Apsos, and Cocker Spaniels on a consistent basis for shampoos and haircuts.

Jackie owned the place. The other full-time staff included groomers, frizzy-haired Lori and shaggy-haired Alan, who had a deadly, expletive-filled vocabulary. The summer before I left for Chapel Hill, Jackie increased my hours so that I could pay for new bed sheets, textbooks, and other items that I needed for school. In August, the staff threw me a going away party complete with a cake. Not everyone went to college and those who did didn't go to a school as prestigious as UNC, so the team was proud of me and a bit wistful.

When one of the customers, a regular, learned about my pending departure, he congratulated me and asked where I was headed.

"UNC Chapel Hill!" I beamed.

The name rolled off my tongue, as I was getting used to saying it.

"Oh, that's great!" he said, his eyebrows raised. "Basketball scholarship?" although, I, all of five feet two inches, had never expressed an interest in playing sports in college.

My enthusiasm, including the sugar high from that celebratory cake, started to deflate like a day's old balloon, not all at once but over time like a car tire with a nail inside of it.

"Fucking asshole!" Alan said when I recounted the story later, his scissors clicking furiously.

"Fast Car," Tracy Chapman
peaked at #6 Hot 100

The bell on the front door chimed.

"Your friend is back," Alan smirked stressing the word friend as though it was in air quotes.

Corey had been stopping by the pet store either on his way to or from his job either as a delivery driver or clerk—I could never remember which. He always had a funny story to share and to re-enact but mostly we talked about nothing in particular. Our off and on romance which began back at G.W. Junior High and peaked with a tortuous triangle between me, him, and Rob had settled into something like friendship, finally.

While I unpacked the latest shipment of Science Diet dog food, dog toys, and overpriced pet shampoos, on this day, I chattered on about UNC, including my dorm assignment and the roommate I was excited to meet. Based on the letters that she sent me, including a grainy photo of her camping with her family, Kimberly seemed really nice.

In turn, Corey told me that his girlfriend of the past year, someone who also graduated in their class a year ahead of me, was expecting twins. Now over 6 feet tall, Corey was a big kid himself, always cracking jokes and play fighting against imaginary enemies using various martial arts styles ("Monkey style!" he would yell in the street after putting me in a fake headlock), so I had a hard time imagining him with not one but two babies.

"I gotta find me another job," Corey said while watching me work my way through the shipment.

"Yeah . . ." I nodded, my mind on the pending major that I needed to choose and the housing deposit I needed to send in. Further, all new first-year students were expected to mail in a photo and information about our hometown, major, and hobbies. It was for the *Class of 1992 Freshman Record*, a thin yearbook but only for new students—an opportunity for us to preview the campus and to get to know one another before the semester begins. But it was also an opportunity for us to brag a little about our accomplishments to date.

I was stumped.

I was told many times that I should go to law school because a) I didn't like science and wouldn't cut it as a doctor and b) I'm "good at talking" and like to write. I heard that studying political science was good for lawyers, so I put that down and listed "people" and "reading" as hobbies.

Corey and I looked down at our respective sneakers as the sounds of the cars outside passed by. The end of my shift was approaching, so we quickly hugged. He headed out the door, and I disassembled the remaining boxes. The door jingled after him.

"My Prerogative," Bobby Brown
peaked at #1 Hot 100, #1 Hot Black Singles

Mom drove me down to Chapel Hill and moved me and all of my Carolina blue items—among them, a comforter, towels, and notebooks—onto the second floor of Avery Hall where we finally met my roommate Kimberly, a curly-haired blonde sophomore from King's Mountain, North Carolina, who was pleasant but also aloof. Mom stayed at a local hotel, but I didn't hesitate to start unpacking and decided determinedly that I would spend the night in my new home.

The next day Mom offered to help out, to check out the campus, to get me settled. But I shooed her away and promised to call often, as she headed towards our car.

Already, I was relieved to be away from her regime—the constant nitpicking and questioning. The sharp tones and constant demands on my time. Between 10th grade and now, things grew tense between us, as we bumped heads on everything from how I styled my hair to what would be a reasonable curfew. I even threatened to run away from home but was thwarted. Mom laughed, mocked me, told me to go ahead, but snapped that I *better not* go to my grandmother's house as a safe harbor.

But I was grown now. I knew how to walk with purpose down busy D.C. streets with my hands in my pockets and not look directly at strangers and not take flyers from anyone. I mastered public transportation, and I could find my way home from any location in the metropolitan area, including Southern Maryland and Northern Virginia.

I had read everything I could find out about the university, and I had been in school my whole life.

Most importantly, she'd never gone to college, and I made it. *I got this*, I told her.

"You're Not My Kind of Girl," New Edition
peaked at #95 Hot 100, #3 R&B Singles

Kimberly stopped talking to me about a month into the semester not long after Mom dropped me off and headed back up Highway 95. We spent the summer writing letters to one another and sending each other photos, but suddenly the atmosphere in our room grew chilly. There seemed to be a competition to see who would break the silence first, and we barely acknowledged one another in our room or in our suite.

I chalked it up to irreconcilable differences, but Mom offered to drive back down 95 and have words with this white girl. I told her that I was fine and simply avoided my room as much as possible. Feeling physically displaced, I searched for places on campus where I felt comfortable and also tried to find kindred spirits among my peers. I sat on the floor of our hallway suite and called Rob, who was a sophomore at George Mason University about four hours away. But what was I going to do? I couldn't stay on the phone with him all day.

To ease the pain, I stared at photographs of Wilmington, North Carolina's pristine beaches and imagined that it is what California—freedom—looked like.

"Something Just Ain't Right," Keith Sweat
peaked at #79 Hot 100, #3 R&B Singles

I had no idea why I was taking biology of all things in my first semester. And with a lab, too. I definitely was not planning to major in one of the sciences but most of my peers were taking the class, so I signed up, as well. But I fell asleep whenever I started studying and was barely scraping by with a D. I didn't know yet that I could drop a class and if I did, I'm not sure that I would. There were only a handful of Black students in the class. I couldn't be the one who quit.

"No Pain, No Gain," Betty Wright
peaked at #14, Hot R&B/Hip-Hop Songs

I had my meals down to a science. I ate French toast with a side of bacon and a splash of syrup in the mornings and a grilled cheese sandwich with a side of fries for dinner. I took a nap in the middle of the day to skip lunch. That was my diet for the entire first semester. At this time, students were charged for every item on our tray, and these were the least expensive items in the dining hall. I typically ate my meals alone to avoid my friends asking me if I was eating grilled cheese *again*.

When my Avery suitemates invited me to join them off-campus for dinner one night, I told them I had a bunch of reading to do and stayed behind.

When Mom asked me how I was doing during one of our weekly calls, I told her, *"Good!"*

"What I Am," Edie Brickell & New Bohemians
peaked at #7 Hot 100

My Black friends started calling me "Tracy Chapman" not only because she was one of my favorite artists at the time but because of how much I listened to her album. When I first arrived on campus, I played "Fast Car" nearly every day on the stereo I brought with me from home. The chords haunted me, and the song reminded me of home, of hope, of past, of present, a close call.

When I was in elementary school, Mom bought me an acoustic guitar for some reason (who knows? Maybe I begged her for it) and there was a period of time when I composed songs out of the poems that I wrote about leaving home and finding my purpose. I'm sure that she offered, but I couldn't be bothered with taking guitar lessons–those would only dilute the purity of my compositions.

With her short natural hair, round apple cheeks, and cocoa brown skin, Chapman looked more like someone in my family than she did like the popular Black female artists of the day most of whom were tall, svelte, and had high octave ranges. Tracy's voice was earnest and sounded a bit wobbly at times like she was nervous and on the verge of crying. When she crooned about feeling like she could be someone (be someone), I felt like Chapman had peered inside of my guts and wrote a song about what she found.

"Only white people listen to this," my new friends laughed, dismissing the acoustic guitar and Chapman's folksy delivery.

After studying the album cover that I displayed in my sacred Carolina blue crate of albums, someone started calling Tracy "Buckwheat" because of her hairstyle.

So, if I = Tracy and Tracy = Buckwheat, then what did that make me? I could do the math.

"Rebel Without a Pause," Public Enemy
uncharted

In place of college advice or large sums of money, Mom sent me care packages in 8x11 envelopes addressed to "La'Tonya R. Rease, Great Poet and Activist" which were meant to inspire me. I placed the glossy black and white postcards and cut out articles from the *Post* next to my pictures of Mike Tyson, Malcolm X, and Rob on my closet door—all three who whispered in my ear to keep going.

To this collection, I added a newspaper clipping of Dale, a controversial graduate student at Carolina who was known for protesting major international injustices like apartheid in South Africa. That year, Nelson Mandela had spent his 70th birthday while in prison and there was a growing anti-apartheid movement on college campuses as many students called for their institutions to divest any financial interests in the country.

I was impressed by Dale's handmade t-shirt that read, "**C**ocaine **I**mporters of **A**merica" that I saw in the *Daily Tar Heel*. Dale was white with spiky hair and round glasses. Rumor had it that he was not even American—maybe that's why he could be so bold with his fashion choices and political statements.

I looked for him whenever I was on main campus, although I wasn't sure what I would say if our paths ever crossed. Would I shake his hand and thank him for his service? Give him a high five and say, "We got this!" Maybe I could ask him if being an activist is a real job that I could get paid for?

What is a graduate student? I wondered to myself.

"Express Yourself," N.W.A.
peaked at #2 Hot Rap Singles, #45 Hot R&B/Hip-Hop Songs

"Do it again!" Darryl from the first floor egged me on with his hat turned around while also sitting backwards at my desk chair.

My fellow Black freshmen—nearly all of whom were from North Carolina and majoring in business—regularly asked me to perform the rap song "Self-Destruction" when we got tired of doing homework because I was the only one in the group who knew all of the lyrics. I also spat songs by Salt-N-

Pepa and Eric B. & Rakim—recited by heart—and demonstrated the karaoke routine of Slick Rick's "Children's Story" that Rob and I perfected before I came to school. I didn't just say the songs; I performed them throwing in dance moves that I saw on The Box music video channel. I put on a one woman show right in my dorm room.

It was moments like these when our differences were the most pronounced, and at times someone kindly reminded me that I was from "up North" and that I was a "Yankee." Having eschewed chemical relaxers starting that summer, I wore my hair in a long, cornrowed ponytail. Over my bed was a large black and white poster of Malcolm X (before the Spike Lee movie) and a red, white, and blue bumper sticker in support of Jesse Jackson for president that declared "Bold Leadership" and a "New Direction" in all caps. Being a Black student at Carolina typically meant getting a degree, landing a good job in order to help bring family along, and not making any waves at school.

Because I could rhyme and I also knew the lyrics to "Fast Car," I often felt as though I was too Black and not Black enough at the same time.

"Don't Worry, Be Happy," Bobby McFerrin peaked at #1 Hot 100, #7 Adult Contemporary, #11 Hot Black Singles

---

During my time at the school, I never watched the Carolina men's basketball team play in Carmichael Auditorium, later renamed the Dean Dome after legendary coach Dean Smith. There was a tradition—a rite of passage almost—for students to camp out overnight to score tickets to a home game, especially when the team played cross-town rival, Duke University.

I had seen those games on television every year—witnessed the Cameron Crazies with their navy-blue face paint and horizontal striped shirts and imagined myself amongst the more genteel UNC fans dressed in long-sleeved button downs and khaki pants. As an official Carolina student, I was no longer an outsider, but I had no interest in going to a game. I told everyone and myself it was because I was really a *Georgetown* fan and never cared much for the Tar Heel team.

One rare night when I had some money, I went out to eat with a handful of friends at the Rathskeller on Franklin Street known for its deep-dish lasagna. I didn't understand why people got so excited about lasagna of all foods, but I went anyway, thinking this was what Mom meant when she told me to have fun in college.

In the darkened restaurant I spotted starting point guard King Rice, caramel colored with a curly high-top fade. He was surrounded by middle-aged white people who wanted to take pictures with him. King smiled patiently while flash bulbs surrounded him like fireworks. Unimpressed, I walked by because I was a Georgetown fan.

"Hand to Mouth," George Michael
uncharted

The Cold War between Kimberly and me ended right before Christmas, ceasing almost as unexpectedly as it started, and we started hanging out a bit more. At times we just sat in our room—her with a towel on her head after taking a shower, me sitting on the edge of my twin bed painting my toenails.

One day after Thanksgiving break, she invited me to join a Secret Santa exchange with her and a group of other sophomores in her class—all white. I felt honored to be invited and was eager to cultivate this fragile relationship with my roommate who also was the first in her family to go to college and was from a town of less than 10,000 people. In a few years, she would become a single mother to Logan, which was extra radical for the time and the location because Logan's biological father was Black.

The spending cap for Secret Santa was $25, and I had approximately $5 dollars in my account. During the fall semester, as I was getting my bearings, I relied on Mom's generosity as she would sometimes include checks inside those care packages that she sent me. I started a typing business in my residence hall to help pay for the long-distance phone bills that I was racking up, and I typically was left with very little spending money after that.

I drew Brent, a popular guy with a warm smile who also wore no-iron button down shirts and ironed dress pants to class. He had been very nice to me, often greeting me with a wide smile and a hug whenever I bumped into him in Avery. I wanted to impress him and to keep the good vibes going. Brent was the kind of white guy that my Black friends told me that we came to college to meet so that we could get good jobs after graduation.

A gift exchange was not in my budget, but I couldn't back out. Over a one- or two-week period, I left Brent a handmade Christmas card made from construction paper using my best handwriting. I had a tiny beige teddy bear that I found from somewhere deep in my desk drawer, and I propped it in front of his dorm room door with a note.

On the night of the final exchange and reveal, we all gathered in someone's room, ate candy, and joked around. My stomach started turning flips as I eyed the large, brightly-colored presents that people held eager to present them to their rightful owners. My cheeks burned as I fingered Brent's present—the only thing I could afford on my fixed income that I felt was worthy of his stature.

The point of Secret Santa was to exchange small gifts all leading to one major present on this very night. Debra, my bubbly suitemate from across the hall, announced herself as my secret Santa and presented me with a 27x40 poster—the largest I've ever seen—of Bob Marley's *Uprising* album cover because she knew how much I loved him. I was elated, and I felt terrible at the same time knowing what was next.

Finally, it was my turn, and the inevitable could no longer be delayed. I looked around the room at my new white friends, all smiles and giddy because of the sugar we were eating and the impending winter break. My eyes landed on Brent, whose grin became wider as he realized that I was the elf leaving him handmade gifts like a little kid trying to please a parent who they only saw on the weekends.

With the remaining money I had left and my bank account close to zero dollars, I splurged. With all eyes on me and the sounds of Christmas tunes playing faintly in the background, I willed myself to cross the room gripping the gift all the while drenched in sweat and shame. I walked up close right under Brent's side so that the present was partially hidden from the witnesses and handed him all that I could offer: a copy of *GQ* magazine that I wrapped really nicely.

SMART GIRL: A FIRST-GEN ORIGIN STORY

"Girl You Know It's True," Milli Vanilli
peaked at #2 Hot 100, #1 Dance Singles, #3 Hot
R&B/Hip-Hop Songs, #1 Hot Rap Songs

At the start of the spring semester, hope sprung anew. I was rejuvenated after the long winter break after hanging out back home with Dani, Kim, and Megan, who attended North Carolina State University, North Carolina A&T, and UVA, respectively.

Marchell, the other Black girl who lived in my suite, and I watched the American Music Awards in her room next door to mine as a much-needed study break. She poked me in the ribs when Tracy Chapman won Favorite Pop/Rock Artist, although Chapman was not present to receive the award.

"Your girrrrl!" Marchell laughed, and I couldn't help but feel vindicated after all of that shit I took from my friends about being a Chapman fan.

We were there for Keith Sweat though. The son of a factory worker and hairdresser, Sweat, it's been told, received a degree in communications from the City College of New York and worked his way up from the mailroom to working as a brokerage assistant. Working on Wall Street was his "day job," but making music was his passion. As fellow Black first-gens, Marchell and I could relate. She was thinking about majoring in business economics for job security, meanwhile, I started wavering on the whole pre-law thing.

Sweat's debut album, *Make It Last Forever*, was a hands down favorite amongst our crew. While my fellow Black classmates raised eyebrows at "Fast Car" and mumbled their way through the day's hip hop hits, we all knew the words to every single song on this album from beginning to end.

As usual, Marchell lay in her bed on the bottom bunk underneath the covers, and I was comfortable on the floor beside her. Our friends floated in and out of the room over the course of the program as they were only invested in the R&B categories and not all of the other genres.

At last, the Favorite Soul/R&B album category. Marchell and I leaned forward at the same time eager for Sweat to pick up his crown. When jazz musician and statesperson George Benson opened the envelope to declare the winner, his eyes went wide.

"George . . . Michael!" he announced.

As the cheers from the TV audience swelled, the dorm room fell silent. Marchell swore and turned off the television.

E185

I had a feeling right away that I wasn't in Northern Virginia anymore.

During freshmen move in at UNC Chapel Hill, I had received an invitation to an afternoon pig pickin' on campus. I called Grandma and demanded an explanation. She chuckled and described what sounded like a positively barbaric practice of a whole pig roasting where people would literally pick the piece that they wanted to eat right off of the animal carcass. I didn't go near that event. This was a foreign concept to me and suggested that while I grew up in the South, I was not *Southern*. I was not expected to say "ma'am" or "sir." I didn't speak with a drawl. And I had never *ever* been to a pig pickin.' Mom didn't even cook pork back home.

The Mason Dixon line divided slave holding states from so-called "free" states and thereby divided the North from the South, with any state below Pennsylvania considered the South. With its proximity to Washington, D.C., which had thousands of transplants from all over the country and the world, Northern Virginia occupied an in-between space. I generally considered myself to be from the mid-Atlantic region, with more in common culturally with Philadelphia and Newark than even Richmond, Virginia, which is 150 miles south in the same state.

But truthfully, these North and South lines weren't as concrete as I'd like to think.

The Franklin and Armfield Slave Pen on Duke Street in Alexandria, less than a mile away from Nana's house, was once one of the largest slave trading stations in the entire nation. From the outside, the building looks like any other row house in Old Town, but between 1828 and 1836, it notoriously housed enslaved Africans who were to be auctioned. Slaves from middle states like Pennsylvania, New York, and New Jersey tended to work on smaller farms or developed specific skills as blacksmiths, coopers, or tailors. In order to increase their revenue, at times slaveholders in these regions would sell their slaves down to places like Louisiana, where they toiled on large plantations under the hot sun picking cotton. The Franklin and Armfield pen in Alexandria was a gateway to the Deep South, the Real South.

But on matters of school desegregation, Virginia aligned itself with Dixie. There is a well-known photograph of Alabama governor George Wallace standing in front of a doorway at the University of Alabama in order to uphold "segregation now, segregation tomorrow, segregation forever" in 1963, but

Wallace's racist policies are built upon a foundation that partly stems from white politicians in Virginia.

In the mid-1950s, Virginia senator Harry Byrd, a Democrat, led Massive Resistance, a statewide pro-segregation campaign that was passed into law in 1956. In 1959, a mere four years after Mom was born, Prince Edward County, Virginia shut down its entire public school system rather than comply with school integration, and it remained closed for the next five years. In other places throughout the state, including Alexandria, Black families had to apply to white public schools and were denied. White families fled to private schools, some which were funded by the state government.

T.C. Williams High School was named after a former superintendent, Thomas Chambliss Williams, a card-carrying white segregationist who openly defied the *Brown vs. Board* decision. The local NAACP took the school board to court and eventually Williams retired in 1963. But de facto segregation simply replaced de jure segregation. Williams's successor, superintendent John Albohm, was a moderate who guided Alexandria toward school integration but who also developed Honors courses and the phase 4 track, the nearly all-white courses I took in high school in the mid to late 1980s, specifically to keep white parents from putting their kids in local private schools like St. Stephens and St. Agnes. Racial segregation persisted within T.C. Williams, no matter how many football games the Titans won.

❋ ❋ ❋

During the fall semester, especially, when I wanted to stay out of my dorm room in Avery Hall as long as possible in order to avoid my roommate Kimberly, I would head to House Undergraduate Library. There were many aspects about being on a college campus that were new to me—rules, policies, and spaces that were wholly unfamiliar and that Mom couldn't help me navigate. But a library, that I had seen before.

Before coming to college, I regularly dawdled in the Lonnie B. Nelson Elementary School library and helped the librarians put books away; I assigned myself a reading challenge one summer and spent most of the day at the Old Town branch in Alexandria reading science fiction; Mom and I sometimes hung out at the MLK library on G Street in D.C. so that she could work on her resume; and, I figured out what colleges to apply to while in the reference section at the Duncan Library near Megan's house. I knew what to expect at a library—where to find books, how to browse a card catalogue.

At House, specifically in the Afro American Studies section, sometimes I would just grab a random book off of the shelf and dig in. Instead of my textbooks, I sat right on the concrete floor and read the autobiographies of Angela Davis and Assata Shakur. I gathered everything I could about the Black Panther Party, as my mind regularly transported me to a magical place called Oakland where a number of significant events took place. All of this Black history and Civil Rights seemed so long ago and so far away, and I wasn't sure if I was a worthy heir. Even my connection with Angela Davis felt tenuous. Davis's father was a proud HBCU graduate, she casually mentioned in her book. And her mother had earned a master's degree. I grasped to find something we had in common.

But I couldn't find stories like my own. There were no books about Black girls from the suburbs who loved sports and hip-hop music. In these texts, only Black manchildren and native sons had basketball heroes or rode the subway to school. I was not facing water hoses or police beatings in the street. I had not been to prison or picked cotton. Maybe my troubles weren't so bad.

❊ ❊ ❊

The day after George Herbert Walker Bush was elected in November 1988, swastikas appeared on campus. Although we students discussed amongst ourselves, I don't recall any campus indictment nor any statement from the university president or even the Dean of Students. The Triangle area—Chapel Hill, Durham, and Raleigh—voted for Dukakis but the state went to Bush, whose campaign manager, Lee Atwater, authorized a race-baiting campaign commercial featuring the mugshot of William "Willie" Horton, a Black man. The swastikas, spraypainted in black almost hurriedly, were like a stamp of approval for Bush.

There were two major debates happening across campus this year: 1) is the minstrel song "Dixie" racist? and 2) is a campus Black Cultural Center an example of <u>reverse</u> racism? The former debate came about after a group of white male students inexplicably burst into song at 11:00 p.m. at House Library. In a letter to the *Daily Tar Heel* editor, Ellen, a first-year student, defended "Dixie," noting that slaveholders were "not all immoral, wicked thugs and the Confederacy was not necessarily the child of sin and humanity." Ellen went on to argue that the Confederacy "was an identity for many Southerners." Singing Dixie stems from "a true loyalty to, love of and pride for the South," Ellen wrote.

By far, the more controversial topic was about a proposed Black Cultural Center. In her written opposition, another first-year student, Tory Palmer, accused Black students of "black racism" and creating their own elite group that was "unaccessible to whites." John Pope, then a member of the University's Board of Trustees, weighed in on the matter as a Guest Writer to the school paper. "My concern," he wrote, "is that the BCC will contribute to re-segregation within the University." He would go on to declare that if Black students wanted the BCC, "maybe they should attend a black university," which outraged us. Pope did not approve of taxpayers' money being used in this way, and the Pope family, under the banner of the John William Pope Foundation, would continue to back conservative public policies in the state under the guise of "individual freedom" and "personal responsibility."

Now a history and Afro American Studies dual major (in my mind only), I wrote in, as well. Fueled by Malcolm X tapes, my philosophy was, if you can't beat 'em, the hell with 'em. Stop begging for acceptance. In a short letter to the editor, I called for Black alumni and Black businesses to fund the BCC since it was clear to me that the campus was unwilling to do so. After writing a few sternly worded memos to my high school principals back at T.C. Williams, I was comfortable fighting my battles on paper, and I fought back the best way I knew how: I joined the writing staff of *The Black Ink*, the official newspaper of the Black Student Movement. I was the only first-year student on the staff.

I also was one out of only 1800 Black students in the total undergraduate population of over 23,500 students and was reminded of my marginality regularly. Greek life was particularly abhorrent, and I dared not venture to or even near Big Frat Court where Black students might suffer any number of indignities. For instance, white fraternity members dumped water and urinated on pledges for Delta Sigma Theta, a historically Black sorority. In another incident, Black sorority members were drenched with water by a white male student as they walked by. These incidents rarely were reported in the campus paper so Black students used the Letter to the Editor section to plead for the university and the Greek system to take a stand and reprimand the perpetrators.

I was furious about these encounters but my classmates often didn't feel the same way. We just needed to get through it. White people ran the world, and we just needed to grab our slice of the pie and get out. Nearly everyone I knew was majoring in either business or economics with the hope of working for a major company and buying a nice house. I, on the other hand, was perceived as a rabble rouser and a disrupter, a Northern muckraker who didn't understand the ways of the South.

Mr. Stanley looked into my eyes and could tell that something was wrong. A middle-aged Black man who reminded me of one of my many great uncles in Williamston, he was the custodian of my residence hall, Avery. Regularly, I would see him as I passed by on my way to the second floor. At first, things started with a casual wave and a polite hello, but then I found myself standing in the doorway of his "office," a darkened room filled with mops, brooms, and buckets, telling him about the D grade I received in biology, a stupid class I had no business taking. I felt bad for keeping him away from his work, but he was the only person who actually <u>asked</u> how I was doing.

"What's up?" he asked.

"I'm thinking about leaving Carolina," I told him one day, something I had not dared to say out loud until that moment.

"Huh," he said, leaning against a mop.

After a pause, he smiled and said that I knew what was best for me. He knew that I was smart and strong.

"If you decide to go, I'll miss you. But I understand," he offered with a wink.

121

Mom had a different response.

"You need to write a report about the pros and cons of transferring" she said into the telephone. "Make a strong argument."

This was a risky proposition. I was only halfway through my first year, and I'd heard that it was common for new students to not feel connected. Additionally, things had taken a turn for the better with Kimberly, and we were pretty close now. When I imagined a future at UNC Chapel Hill, I thought maybe I would join a historically Black sorority, like the girls I saw on campus wearing bright red tams and long overcoats. But I wasn't *excited*. I felt like I was settling and just getting by.

That January, a group of friends and I attended a basketball game held on our campus featuring local HBCUs, North Carolina A&T University and North Carolina Central College. This was my first (and only) time in this stadium. The atmosphere was electric. The school bands each played local radio hits, and it seemed like the entire crowd knew the latest dances like the Roger Rabbit and did them right in the stands. At one point a guy sitting near us got into a friendly ribbing exchange with another guy from the rival losing team. Sharp words were exchanged, but it was all in good fun.

And then there were the cheerleaders. We sat only a few rows in front of the Gold Squad, A&T's lead team, kind of like a varsity squad. The group tumbled and performed stunts, but I couldn't take my eyes away from their high knees, light toes, and rhythmic stomps, or the way that they quickly swiveled their hips, all accompanied by throaty chants repeated over and over. Some students cheered for the cheerleaders and called out an occasional high pitched "Eyupppp." Some of the cheerleaders smiled, most didn't, but every one of them made direct eye contact with the crowd. This was serious business, and you know they meant it when they declared "Aggie PRIDE!"

My muscle memory started kicking in. Although I had denounced cheerleading back in high school, my heart skipped a beat as I watched the Gold Squad. I started mouthing the cheers and couldn't help but stomp along with them. I wasn't an Aggie, but I didn't truly feel like a Tar Heel, either. My heart pulled in a new direction, and suddenly I knew what I needed to do next.

During the fall semester especially, the Black Student Movement hosted notable events on campus. For instance, Washington, D.C. Go-Go band, Experience Unlimited, performed their popular hit "Da Butt" during a brief concert. Spike Lee signed my flyer when he came to Carolina to talk about making *School Daze*. And we also heard a lecture from Civil Rights activist Julian Bond. But these events were sporadic and too few and far between. After the visitors left, we would return to our regular grind of getting by and dodging racist acts lodged by our white peers.

While I briefly considered Wesleyan College in Connecticut, I set my sights on transferring to a HBCU. As per the agreement that I made with Mom, I met with my writing composition instructor and told her that I wanted to submit my final argumentative essay on the importance of attending a historically Black college or university at this time. I referenced newly-published articles in *Newsweek* and *Ebony* magazines that were documenting this resurgence of interest. I received an A.

I departed from UNC Chapel Hill on May 3, 1989. But before I left, I stopped by to see Mr. Stanley one last time, as he was cleaning up all of the mess that we students made during move out. I gave him a thank you card. We didn't talk much, but I hugged him a little tighter for a few seconds longer.

❖ ❖ ❖

As a joke, during senior year of high school, Megan drew a picture of me on torn notebook paper and stapled it inside my T.C. Williams yearbook. It depicts me being strung up on a tree with two cigarette-smoking and alcohol drinking Ku Klux Klan members in hoods nearby who presumably are UNC students. To emphasize her point, she wrote my name and drew an arrow pointing to my swinging body, the face colored in with ink. It is titled, "Party Scene at UNC." I could have drawn the same picture in *her* yearbook and subbed in "UVA," where she attended and the place, during this same academic year, where "Niggers go home" was scrawled upon

Beta Bridge and where members of Phi Gamma Delta fraternity distributed a party flyer with Black characters wearing grass skirts. No "short wops" and "please, no nega babes," it proclaimed.

This was the price of admission. There were things we as Black students were supposed to expect and accept by attending a PWI. We were told to deal with racism—both macro- and micro-aggressions—in college before we went out into the "real world" and worked for companies like Proctor & Gamble where we wouldn't be coddled.

Although I did not have much proof otherwise, I felt like there was something else out there, some other experience to be gained in college besides suffering and pointing out racism to administrators who didn't seem to care. My Black freshman clique, Marchell included, begged me not to leave UNC.

"Stay," they said. "We have so much to learn from you!" referring to my Malcolm X poster and Jesse Jackson bumper sticker.

But I came to college to learn, not to teach, and I just wanted to be a regular 18-year-old, not a lecturer.

I did not know that I was a "first-generation college student," but I did know that I was a Black student, so ultimately, I decided to transfer to the Blackest university in the Blackest city.

NATIVE TONGUES

It had been another long day. We often stayed on The Yard for hours to avoid going back and forth on the shuttle in between classes. Sometimes I grabbed a quick snack at Punchout to kill time or hung out on the steps of Douglass Hall talking to classmates. Other times I would venture over to nearby Georgia Avenue to get some wings with mumbo sauce, greeting all of the street vendors selling incense and Kente cloth as I walked by, the speeches of Malcolm X blasting on large boom box radios.

Meridian Hill and Park Square residence halls were only about a mile away from the main campus, but no one wanted to make that walk. We settled into the campus shuttle for the quick ride, instead.

Lalania sat in a seat in front of me. Like me, she was a transfer student, and she completed three semesters at the University of Wisconsin at Stevens Point, where there was a grand total of 19 Black students. I didn't even know that Black people lived in Wisconsin.

"Did you hear about this guy, Sean?" she asked me, her eyes wide.

I shook my head to clear my mind of the running list of things I needed to do once I got back to my room.

"What about him?"

Lalania clutched the seat. "He has an internship . . . in New York!"

"What do you mean? Like, *right now*?" My brows furrowed in confusion.

She nodded. "Apparently, it was too good to pass up. He's working for a record company so that he can get his foot in the door. But he has to take a train there, like, an actual train!"

We all knew the importance of having an internship as an undergraduate student. No matter the major, our professors told us that we needed to gain experience in whatever field we were interested in, even if that meant doing something for free. But why in the world would anyone make a four-hour commute—each way!—for an unpaid internship? I couldn't fathom putting in all of that work and, presumably, paying for transportation out of pocket for something that wasn't even guaranteed. Seemed like a big risk for Sean, a business major whom people called "Puffy" for some reason.

"That's crazy. What a dummy," I said and looked back out the window as the bus rolled past the Lower Quad, the hospital, and the main gates of The Mecca, Howard University.

❈ ❈ ❈

During my senior year of high school, Rob and I went with a group of friends to see Spike Lee's second movie *School Daze*, which focused on a fictitious historically Black college in Atlanta, Georgia. The film was groundbreaking for its representation of an all-Black college culture in mass media. I liked it well enough, especially the soundtrack, but there was still a disconnect for me. Although the characters were in college, they all seemed much older than us. Additionally, most of the characters were in some way connected to a fraternity, and I was puzzled by the traditions and the lingo: what was a Dean of Pledges? What did it mean to be "on line"? These were new concepts to me.

Just like being a member of the Black Panther Party or a participant in a Civil Rights march, attending Howard University seemed unattainable to me. I knew the school was in Washington, D.C., but like Georgetown, I had never visited the campus and never ever considered it a real option when I was applying for schools, partly because the guidance counselors and some of the teachers described HBCUs, places like Virginia State and Norfolk State, as "13th grade" and not a place to go if you were really smart. In fact, they weren't even referred to as HBCUs—just "Black schools," said with a sneer that implied that they were inferior.

But while I was still at Chapel Hill making decisions about where to transfer and take my talents, I heard about thousands of Howard students who took over the Mordecai Wyatt Johnson Administration (or "A") Building for three days. The appointment of Republican National Chairman, Lee Atwater, the same man who oversaw George Bush's election campaign, to the university's board of trustees was one catalyst for this protest. In addition to Atwater's immediate removal, students demanded a more Afrocentric curriculum, better campus security, and more efficient financial aid processing as the school's bureaucracy was notoriously confusing at best and unhelpful at worst, causing needless delays and dropped classes.

I told Mom, *This is where I need to be.* I felt called to the Mecca to join other like-minded activists who were not in a history book but alive and also my age.

By far, the most crowded shuttle from campus was the Thursday 7:30 p.m. bus—that was the last one you could take to make it to your room in time to watch the appetizer, "The Cosby Show," at 8:00 p.m., which preceded our main course, "A Different World," which aired a half hour later. Like *School Daze*, "A Different World" also was set at a Southern HBCU, Hillman College, which we all knew for certain was a stand in for Howard, especially since Debbie Allen, esteemed Howard graduate, took over as producer and lead director during the second season. I typically watched the show with Lalania and her roommates in the all-women's residence hall, Park Square. We felt giddy watching a TV version of our school each week but also a little smug knowing that our real experience was even better.

My fellow Bison at this time included: Student Body Vice President and future Newark mayor, Ras Baraka (son of poet and Howard alumnus, Amiri Baraka); future Atlanta mayor, Kasim Reed; Garfield Bright, Marc Gay, Carl Martin, and Darnell Van Rensalier, who formed the R&B group, Shai; Carl Anthony Payne, who was juggling school while playing "Cockroach" on "The Cosby Show"; future president of Virginia State University, Makola Abdullah; my one-time residential building mate Tracy Wilson who was dating Georgetown basketball star, Alonzo Mourning; future Black TV show staple, Wendy Raquel Robinson, who graduated *cum laude*; actor Anthony Anderson, who left school during his junior year due to financial difficulties but would return almost 30 years later to complete his degree; journalism major and classmate Karen Good, who was only a few years away from editing for *Vibe* and *honey* magazines; and, Sean "Puffy" Combs, who converted that unpaid internship into a full-time job at Uptown Records.

It was not uncommon for popular Black artists like Heavy D. and The Boys or members of Bell Biv Devoe to hang out on The Yard when they were in town. New Jack Swing group Guy performed on campus, and the ever-popular Keith Sweat escorted our Homecoming Queen across Greene Stadium at halftime.

After dropping out of school, Puffy made a triumphant return to campus during fall 1991 to showcase his new act, an R&B group that he was grooming in his likeness. Lalania,

Rob, and I were excited to see Boyz II Men up close at Cramton Auditorium and, resplendent in our baggy jeans and oversized shirts, we waited in line a long time to see them. The opening act was Puffy's proteges, Jodeci, that had a hit on the radio, "Forever My Lady." Unlike the nerdy cool aesthetic of Boyz II Men, who looked more like affable fraternity members, these four guys, dressed in matching denim outfits with baseball caps turned backwards, looked like and acted like thugs but sang like choir boys. One of them—the scrawniest—grabbed a young woman in the front row by the back of her head and rubbed her face into his crotch while he belted into the microphone. The crowd didn't know whether to boo or to cheer.

Our youthful look and vibe, filled with brightly patterned rayon shirts, polka dots, and African-inspired medallions, was everywhere—not just on "A Different World"—but other places on television. We could see images of ourselves amongst the University of Michigan Fab Five and the NCAA champion UNLV men's basketball team. Even if they weren't college students, many contemporary hip-hop artists, including A Tribe Called Quest, Monie Love, De La Soul, Queen Latifah, and Naughty By Nature were college-aged and looked and dressed like us. Shaw University students Lords of the Underground filmed one of their music videos at their alma mater; TLC's "Baby Baby Baby" took place at an unnamed HBCU and was filmed at Bowie State University; and our very own Shai lobbied for their third video, "Baby I'm Yours," to take place at Howard.

The summer before I started Howard University, I cut all of my hair and wore it in a high-top fade, ironically, not unlike the style worn by one of the *School Daze* stars, who played a Jigaboo. With my part-time job at Marianne Store downtown on G Street, I was able to afford a wardrobe filled with lime green and grape purple outfits, along with a drawer full of patterned hosiery with designs running up the back of the leg.

Although our house in Clinton, Maryland was only 16 miles away, it made more sense for me to live on campus. My Volkswagen Kirby was no longer operational and there was no viable public transportation to D.C. There was a promise of the Green Line metro station that would connect Prince George's County, where Mom lived, to Howard University and the Shaw District, but every time I checked the Metro map, I only saw dashes where the future station *would be*. As a result, I didn't go home too often.

Although I didn't join any formal campus clubs, I immersed myself into campus life, hanging out with a range of people like Lalania, who was not allowed to eat sugar as a kid and grew up without a TV in her Wisconsin home, and New York Mike who got upset, cursed you out, and stormed out of the dorm room if you underbid during Spades.

We were often told that a Black college or university wasn't "the real world," and that a predominantly white institution, like UNC Chapel Hill, would better prepare us for the workforce. But with race pretty much off the table, I encountered a wide variety of people at Howard, like the New York City contingent who booed all of the homecoming performers no matter how good they were; the boho Californians who dressed differently and had different slang than the rest of us; the West Indians and the Black African immigrants; and there were College Republicans, Black N.I.A. Force, and the Fruit of Islam on campus. Just like at UNC, there was a fair number of business majors at Howard but there was also a critical mass of people who studied fine art and zoology. Broadcast and print journalism were also popular majors, as many people, including fellow student Malaak Compton (future spouse of Chris Rock), believed that the arts could make a difference.

❀ ❀ ❀

Disproving my belief that all Black people lived either on the East Coast, in the South, or in Oakland, I met Nicole, a classmate from Anchorage, Alaska. We struck up a friendship in one or two Afro American Studies courses. This was 1991 and Operation Desert Storm was lurking. Although it was a military offense, in other words, a war, most people, especially young people, were not following the news because it was called "Operation Desert Storm," a benign term. There was not the same concern as there had been for the Vietnam War, for instance.

But I was paying attention and following the news closely. After his sophomore year at George Mason University, Rob and a classmate, James, decided to sign up for the Marine Corps reserves to help pay for school since he was covering his own expenses entirely. Rob also was facing academic probation and felt like he could use some discipline. Three months after he returned from boot camp in South Carolina, while I was at my first year at Howard, Rob received word that he, but not James, would be deployed to Kuwait driving artillery. He had no strong pro-military beliefs and no anti-Saddam Hussein feelings. He simply needed to pay for school and get his life on track, and now he was being sent to fight overseas at age 22.

Can you support the soldier and not support the war? That was a powerful question that Juan Williams, a *Washington Post* writer, posed. I decided that I could do both. In the letters that I sent to Rob, I included homemade tapes of Public Enemy and X-Clan so that he wouldn't be brainwashed by the military. I even mailed him a tiny Pan-African flag until he told me to cut it out because the government was scanning all of their mail.

Along with a small group of other students, Nicole and I formed an anti-war organization called the Student Liberation Action Movement, or S.L.A.M. Our goals were to raise campus awareness about the Persian Gulf War, especially given the inequitable number of Black men, like Rob, being deployed. We wanted to shake up the sleepy campus and get our fellow students to see the big picture. In early February of this year, we joined college students all over the country, including the University of Michigan and Columbia University, on a day of protests against the war. Our group, along with members of Black N.I.A. Force, the organization who took over the Administration Building in March 1989, coordinated a teach-in at Douglass Hall, with support from faculty members in English, political science, and economics.

Although the coverage in the *Washington Post* described the national student protests as "light" and "faint," I felt like we were making a difference. We were raising awareness, disrupting the usual humdrum on campus, and getting involved in the *real world*. In comparison, administrators told students at the Other HU (Hampton University) that they would not graduate if they protested President George Bush's presence at their upcoming commencement. Students also were not allowed to wear Kente cloth to graduation, and they had a campus policy where demonstrations had to be pre-approved or students could potentially lose their financial aid if they participated in so-called "illegal" demonstrations. We Bison reveled in our protest tradition and turned up our noses at those Uncle Toms down in Hampton.

Under Nicole's leadership, S.L.A.M. continued to pressure the Howard administration to take a position against the war. One unassuming Friday afternoon, while Black N.I.A. Force led a public demonstration outside of Douglass Hall, we S.L.A.M.

members stealthily ran to the flagpole in the middle of the yard, in broad daylight, disassembled it, and lit the American flag on fire. As we made our getaway, I stumbled and fell, my glasses flying a yard or two ahead of me. I grabbed them and ran blindly behind my fellow protestors. I could barely make out the soles of their boots. Our classmates debated whether the flag burning was a smart thing to do, and a *Hilltop* writer referred to us as "guerilla activists," but S.L.A.M. never took credit for the act choosing instead to remain anonymous.

Arguably, our most bold act was a carefully planned silent "death march" meant to draw attention to the seriousness of the war. Our core group members wore all black pants and long-sleeved shirts, black boots, and white masks. I also wore a red bandana to completely cover my hair. Four of us walked across campus, making our way slowly, one significant step at a time, through Locke Hall, Douglass Hall, and Blackburn Center. One person beat a large drum, two others carried a white body bag ("Black contribution to the New World Order" written on it), and I led the way in the front, holding a gray makeshift tombstone that read: HU: Where Do You Stand?

Our ultimate destination was the Administration building where we asked to meet with new president Franklyn Jenifer. President Jenifer kindly sat down with us in his office and listened to Nicole explain passionately why Howard University needed to be at the forefront of the anti-war movement. He said that he understood and would look into it. About two weeks later, the war ended, and Rob came home.

❦ ❦ ❦

As I approached the end of my junior year, I started to give serious thought about my next step after graduation. Without formally declaring it or speaking to an academic advisor, I changed my major (in my mind only) to Afro American Studies and also added English as a minor. I started to imagine myself as a teacher, like my favorite high school instructor, Ms. Nancy Lyall, who taught the first ever Black Experience in the United States course back at T.C. Williams. I heard that I needed a master's degree in order to teach, so I started looking into that.

A whole master's degree! I thought to myself getting giddy at the thought.

By chance, I came across a brightly colored flyer in the hallway of Locke Hall. "Are You Interested in Graduate School?" it asked. I was interested, but what stood out the most was the opportunity to be <u>paid</u> each semester and over the summer for doing research, which I thought only science majors could do. By this time, I had a 3.7 grade point average and was in the College of Arts and Sciences Honors Program with an academic scholarship that covered my tuition. I snatched the flyer from the bulletin board and stuffed it in my backpack so that no one else could see this opportunity.

About six months before Len Bias died at the University of Maryland, I, along with millions of others, watched in horror the morning of January 28, 1986, while the Space Shuttle *Challenger* disintegrated before our eyes on television. We heard a lot about this particular mission in school especially because a civilian teacher, Christa McAuliffe, was among the crew. Also among them, often appearing discreetly in the background or on the far right of most publicity photos was Ronald E. McNair, an astronaut, physicist, and Black man. In his honor, members of Congress established the Ronald E. McNair Post-Baccalaureate Achievement Program three years later with the ambitious goal of preparing "underrepresented and first-gen + low-income students" for doctoral programs in order to create more diversity among professors.

Located a little more than four miles away from Howard University, American University was among the first 14 institutions nationally to receive funding, and the program recruited students from local schools, including Howard, Catholic University, and George Mason University. Just over 20 of us met once a month on Saturdays on the American University campus, as we learned about the differences between a master's degree and a doctorate, as well as quantitative versus qualitative research, and we discussed the GRE.

What struck me most was research. I simply could not believe that we could get paid to read and learn about something that we were interested in. I wanted to know how the Southern accent developed? Every Black person I knew claimed to be part Native American—how did that come to be? Why were there suddenly so many contemporary movies about Black life but nearly all of them took place in "the hood"? The program reminded me of my GATE days in South Carolina when I would leave my home school and travel across town to another institution for supplemental instruction. But this time, everyone was Black or Latino. Our group felt special, like X-Men.

Our Professor X, Rhonda, actually was a master's student studying social welfare in Baltimore. As the program coordinator, she was responsible for the curriculum, and one day asked us to list all of the people we personally knew who had a Ph.D. and was <u>not</u> one of our professors. I was stumped. How in the world would I meet such a person outside of a classroom, I wondered. Were there Ph.D. holding people just walking around in the wild? I left my paper blank.

As was required for McNair, I applied for an eight-week residential summer research program at the University of Maryland at College Park. I requested to work for the Afro American Studies Program, which was chaired by Black economist Samuel L. Myers, Jr. Although not technically an internship, this was an opportunity for me to test if I was really serious about this discipline and to meet more people who had Ph.D.s. As I learned more about graduate programs, I imagined that I would earn my Master's—the first in the family!—at a place like Morgan State University, another HBCU, or the University of Maryland campus all the way in Baltimore before settling down in my own two story, four-bedroom house in the southern Maryland suburbs, maybe in a place like Silver Spring.

With only three semesters left before graduation and my future looming bright, sometimes in between classes I would just sit in Founders Library, one of the most recognizable buildings on campus, and read Nikki Giovanni's poetry and attempt my own. Designed by Black architect Albert Cassell, the library houses the world-renowned Moorland-Spingarn Research Center. The School of Law used to be located in Founders Library, and the plaintiff attorneys for the 1954 *Brown v. Board of Education* case, including future Supreme Court Justice Thurgood Marshall, practiced in this building. The sense of history was palpable. When I was at UNC, I sat on the hard floor of the library and read about the titans of Civil Rights. Here, I believed that my involvement with S.L.A.M. and my participation in the McNair Scholars Program may have been small pebbles in the ocean but they would nonetheless have a ripple effect someday even if only on campus or in my family.

Occasionally, I would pay a visit to Dr. Russell Adams, then chair of the Afro American Studies Department, which was located in the library, during his office hours to hear a tale about Malcolm X or just to hear his rumbling voice, which had aged to perfection. Sometimes I would interrupt

Ethelbert Miller, who directed the African American Studies Resource Center, while he was trying to eat his lunch in peace. I pshawed when he told me that he was a famous poet in his own right. Quiet and humble Ethelbert a published writer? The Washington, D.C. mayor had even named a day after him. No way. He just shook his head and chuckled when I expressed my amazement and then I bounced away and through the heavy front doors and onto the Yard, my backpack heavy with novels that I needed to read for class.

No matter where I sat on campus, I could hear the bells ring from the library clock tower.

Here was peace.

STUDY LONG

Twenty two was the magic number.

That was the number of Founders I knew I had to eventually memorize if I was going to be a member of this sorority that originated on Howard University's campus.

Osceola McCarthy Adams, Marguerite Young Alexander, Winona Cargile Alexander . . .

I started chanting the names to myself while in the shower and brushing my teeth.

I had some vague idea about this organization. I had seen small elephant figurines in Mrs. Barnwell's office back at T.C. Williams and knew that she was in the sisterhood. And I recalled that the white fraternity boys at Carolina disrupted the sorority's precious outdoor ritual with their racist taunts. I was intrigued, especially knowing that women like Shirley Chisholm, Nikki Giovanni, and Mary McLeod Bethune were members. At times, people more knowing than I would give me a long look, nod, and say that they definitely could see me in this sorority given the organization's commitment to sisterhood, scholarship, and service.

At Howard, I had a few classes in Just Hall and could see the looming yet graceful twelve-and-a-half-foot tall Lady Fortitude statue just outside of the window. I dared not ask directly but I learned that it was connected to this organization. There were other art pieces on campus, as well, that were tied to other fraternities and sororities—some subtle, unassuming, and almost hidden in the ground while others more obvious—that piqued my interest. From across the Yard, I could see Greek letters and colors painted on trees. I nearly stumbled on a discrete plot that suddenly appeared out of nowhere in the grass. I couldn't ask anyone about them though, just heard that we were not allowed to touch them unless we were a member. I stayed away to be safe.

When word spread that the organization was having a fall informational meeting for prospective members during my junior year, I decided to take a chance. But I learned quickly that I was not supposed to ask anyone about this meeting or risk being *too interested* and thereby ruled out from joining. I heard from other girls that we were not supposed to wear red, white, black, pink, green, blue, or yellow to this event, the combined colors of not only this sorority but all of the others on campus, and thereby ruled out from joining for being both too presumptuous and too stupid to know better. That left me with a brown and purple sweater combination, which I hoped signaled just the right amount of interest and situational awareness.

My suitemate D'Angela went with me, and we joined hundreds of girls in this quest. The throng entered a large reception hall on the second floor of Blackburn University Center. Flanked on either side of us were the divine sorority members—all dressed in black. Most of them had stoic faces and already seemed unimpressed with us hopefuls. I fixated on Shauna, the one who smiled the most and looked like the friendliest. Over the course of the afternoon, we heard from current members whose biological sisters, mothers, and even *grandmothers* were sorors. One of my grandmothers had married young and started having kids—nine of them—right away. The other had kids young but was a single parent for a long time. I doubted that college was ever an option for Nana or Grandma, much less joining a prestigious sorority.

These women, I would come to learn, were considered legacies. The prospectives who had a lineage or connection to the organization moved through the crowd with ease. They made small talk and balanced their drinks and appetizers casually. I understood that I was supposed to get to know the Big Sisters, but I couldn't bring myself to do it. I was torn and, as a result, frozen in my indecision. On the one hand, I told myself, *This is why you're here*. To take advantage of these opportunities. To keep running the race and to eventually cross the finish line. But there was another voice, one that was more like an insistent whisper than a shout, that told me, *You do not belong here*. They may look like you, but these are not your people.

Sunni Acoli-Squire was there. Not only was her father a legendary member of the Black Panther Party and compatriot of my hero, Assata Shakur, Mr. Acoli-Squire graduated from Prairie View A&M with a mathematics degree at age 19. What could I possibly say to her without looking dumb? I made a smile that was more like a grimace when I walked by her. The ice in my now sweaty plastic cup melted, as I stayed close to D'Angela, who was two full years younger than me, and I barely spoke to anyone else, actively avoiding anyone wearing all-black.

I prepped for this event the only way that I knew how: by studying. I pored over a published history of the organization and began memorizing the Founders. I scoured the previous year's school yearbook, and I looked for every sorority member in those pages and framed her picture with a yellow highlighter marker. I learned their names, majors, and co-curricular activities. This research-based approach was how I conquered that teacher baby picture contest back in junior high school and won that gift certificate to Kemp Mill Records. It was what I knew how to do—put my head down, don't ask questions, and just figure it out on my own. I didn't know that there was another set of skills required, something a little less tangible, that many of the other girls seemed to grasp.

By the end of the hour, I came to the conclusion that I was not in the right place and that perhaps I had crossed into a multiverse where my superpowers didn't work. I began to realize that the sense of belonging here followed rules I could not read. Those red and white jackets that the sorority members wore, so familiar at first glance, now seemed like symbols in a secret language, the kind written in invisible ink.

LONG DIVISION

Solve this problem.

> A smart Black girl is determined to finish college. She starts her journey at an HBCU but faces multiple financial obstacles along the way. She works various jobs but struggles to save enough to cover her expenses.
>
> Given the following variables:
> - Grit (G): 100%
> - Financial Support (F): 0-10%
>
> How long will it take for her to finish college? Show your work!

The fall of my junior year at Howard University, I started receiving notices about a housing bill for my time spent in Park Square Residential Hall as a sophomore transfer. I started to dread those flimsy papers that appeared in my campus mailbox to the point where I would walk right by the Meridian Hill front desk avoiding the mail altogether. The current year was all paid up, but my eyes shifted from left to right where I saw in Courier font what I owed the housing office from the previous year.

It was a four-figure amount.

I had to come up with a plan.

I calculated that after all of my expenses, including:

- **groceries** because I could not afford a meal plan and had to cook surreptitiously using a portable stove in my room, standing near the open window so that the smell would drift outside and not down the hallway

- a **telephone bill**

- **bus fare and a Metro card** to work, my internships, or the McNair program at American University across town

- an **occasional treat** like Popeye's chicken

- a **periodic haircut** because growing my hair out would take even more time and money that I did not have; and

- **credit card debt** that I accumulated during my freshman year buying sneakers and clothes for my little cousin Monique who was headed to college soon

but excluding:

- **most of my textbooks** that cost more than $20.00

I could bring down my housing bill in just under two years.

I did not tell Mom.

I remembered how nervous I was when she sent me a $600+ check that I had to hand over to the UNC-Chapel Hill bursar—or was it the registrar?—to pay for the spring semester of my freshman year. It was the largest amount of money I had ever seen written on a personal check. How in the world could she afford that on her own working as an administrative assistant?

Besides, Mom had quit that job by now and gone all in on her own business venture and had a mortgage to pay. I didn't want to bring another complication to her, and this Howard bill was much bigger than that.

I decided that this was one problem that I needed to figure out on my own.

Out of the blue, Nana sent me a check to help out. I stared at it for a long time, not sure how to assess it. I knew that I needed to pay for housing, but I also needed to eat, but I also needed a place to live. Therein lay the conundrum.

I made more than a minimum payment to Visa—for once!—and paid $50.00 to Howard University as an act of good faith. I saved the rest for emergencies (meaning: food and transportation).

"You cannot apply current financial aid to a past balance." This logic made zero sense to me.

Thanks to my high grade point average, I earned an academic scholarship that covered my expenses for the current year. The issue was the lingering housing balance from the year prior, which loomed over my head like a nimbostratus cloud.

My Howard bestie Lalania encouraged me to speak with Dean Alvin Thornton, her Constitutional Law professor who I had seen often in the hallways of Douglass Hall. We didn't exactly know what a dean was, but we knew his title meant that he might be able to do something about the situation.

Within the privacy of his office, I explained the problem to Dr. Thornton. He wanted to help and graciously offered to award me an additional scholarship to cover the balance.

But when I gave this fantastic news to the person behind the counter at the Administration Building, I was told the same thing repeatedly, sometimes quickly and sometimes slowly, as though English was not my first language:

"You cannot apply current financial aid to a past balance."

The additional scholarship would change nothing.

I reported this obtuse information to Dr. Thornton, a working-class country boy who was raised in Roanoke, Alabama; who attended segregated public schools in Randolph County; who earned his undergraduate degree from Morehouse College and was inspired by then president Dr. Benjamin E. Mays; who earned a Ph.D. in political science from Howard University; who worked as a legislative aide to Congressman John Conyers, Jr.; who would go on to become Associate Provost at Howard and chair of the Prince George's County Public Schools Board of Education; and who could not figure this out, either.

I knew something didn't add up as soon as Lalania and I approached the door to my room at the end of the hallway in

Meridian Hall. Everyone agreed that I had the best set-up in the building. My assigned roommate never showed up, and I had a room all to myself but was charged for a double and not a single, which made the cost even lower. I shared a suite that was meant for four people total with only one other person, D'Angela. It was a corner room with a view of 16th Street and the Adams Morgan neighborhood just beyond to the west.

As I stood in front of the door, my eyes zeroed in on a small metal gadget that was inside the keyhole. My dorm key could not fit inside of it, nevertheless I kept trying to insert it, hoping for a different result. I didn't even see the paper notice on the door at first.

I could hear Lalania saying something to me, although it sounded from miles away. Her voice was getting shaky and rising higher—that much I could tell.

All I could compute at the moment was: *My stuff is in there.*

How was I supposed to get everything out and find a new place to live within 24 hours?

When I was in elementary school back in Columbia, South Carolina, I was obsessed with playing pinball. It helped, of course, that my teen idol, Brooke Shields, starred in a movie as a young pinball playing genius. But the game itself fascinated me: how even though you could pull the plunger with the same amount of tension and push the flipper buttons with the same amount of effort and how the ball, governed by the rules of gravity, may follow the same path along the course, you never know where the ball will end up. Things may start off well enough, and you can shift—or tilt—the machine with your hip, and you may have a lot of confidence as that shiny metal ball bounces feverishly between bumpers while the points rack up that this will be a long game, but then suddenly, inexplicably, the ball rolls right between the flippers without warning.

The point at which stability moves to instability. That is chaos theory.

A Meridian Hill staff member opened my dorm room long enough for me to gather as much of my belongings as I could in trash bags and crates: my Prince albums and posters, all of my paperbacks, stuffed animals that Rob had given me as Valentine's Day presents, the S.L.A.M. tombstone that I gripped during the death march, which was only two months ago but seemed like two years had passed. Some things I took over to Lalania's, some Rob drove to Mom's house in Maryland, and some I gave to my suitemate D'Angela to thank her for the good memories.

I dared not say anything to my family back in Alexandria. After all, I was the Golden Child—the one who was supposed to make it, the one whom everyone else pinned their hopes on. If I couldn't get through school, who could? At this time, I was helping my cousin, Monique, another smart girl, make her way through T.C. Williams High School and on to college. I took her on college visits, made sure that she was enrolled in the right classes, and confirmed that Mrs. Barnwell was her guidance counselor. I was the Big Cousin, the Almost Sister, and it was my job to make sure that she and all of the others were okay. How was I supposed to look her in the eye and tell her that I couldn't even do it?

Although I appreciated Lalania's offer, I only crashed at her place for a few nights. She already had several roommates, and I didn't want to bother anyone or impose on them during this time of the year. Or ever.

I also couldn't return to my home in Maryland because I didn't have a way to campus, and final exams were two weeks away. Thanks to a tip I heard from another student, I rented a cheap temporary room at an older alum's house in LeDroit Park, near the south end of campus. There were other students staying there, but I barely saw them. We just nodded at one another if we happened to see each other in the hallway or on the stairs. It was just a place for me to lay my head with enough space for me to have some clothes and a few books. I just needed to write the paper for Dr. Adams's class and finish the semester.

I earned nearly a 4.0 that term.

But I never received those grades.

My spring registration was now considered "invalidated" and all student activity was blocked. Not only did those grades not count, I could not access my official transcripts —that column of As with an occasional B here and there— from the past two years either.

With my transcript being withheld for a ransom that I could not pay, if I wanted to transfer to another school, which I didn't, I would reset as a new sophomore somewhere else and add even more time to a degree. I was two semesters and a summer session away from graduation.

It made sense to me that paying off the balance and somehow lowering my expenses was > starting over.

Mom told me that I received a letter from the University of Maryland notifying me that I had been admitted to the prestigious summer research program that I applied for as required of the McNair Program. The letter forecasted my ability to work alongside esteemed, world-renowned tenured faculty; mentioned the well-stocked library, special collections, and research materials; described the world-class campus recreational facilities; and raved about weekly enrichment activities in Washington, D.C. I would be able to share ideas with like-minded peers from all of the country and present the results of my research at a symposium at the end of the summer.

In sum, I thought: I will have free housing and meals for two months. That will give me enough time to figure things out.

"La'Tonya, why aren't you in school?"

Carla Gary's question stopped me mid-sentence as she breezed past my desk on her way to Dr. Harley's office. Her voice was casual, but the words cut deeper than she probably intended.

By then, over a year had passed since I first arrived at the University of Maryland for what I thought would be a temporary summer research program. I entered that summer believing it would be the bridge to solve for x: the unpaid housing balance at Howard University that loomed like a divisor threatening to break my future into smaller, less manageable pieces. Instead, one season multiplied into another, and I found myself trapped in an unbalanced equation, settling into the routine of full-time work without ever simplifying the problem I set out to solve.

On the surface, things looked fine—I was surrounded by the hum of campus life, spent evenings in the university's well-stocked library, and even presented my summer research findings to peers. But beneath it all, I was trapped. The problem hadn't disappeared. No scholarship appeared out of nowhere. No generous benefactor arrived to wipe the slate clean. I still owed Howard University. And every day that passed, the distance between where I was and where I wanted to be felt more insurmountable.

At the conclusion of the summer program, Dr. Sharon Harley, a faculty member in the Afro American Studies Program, asked about my plans: was I considering graduate school? Was I thinking about a Ph.D., like the one she had earned in history at Howard University? I explained my complication. After a pause, she told me that Ramona, the current administrative assistant for the Afro American Studies Program (or AASP), was leaving for law school.

"Why don't you work here and save money until you can go back to Howard?"

Having helped Mom at her old job as an administrative assistant and having worked at the pet store back in high school, I was familiar with how to greet visitors and how to properly answer telephones. My additional responsibilities at AASP, at least initially, included typing memos and scheduling appointments for Dr. Myers who was my faculty advisor for that summer research program and the program chair. I earned a little more money on the side as a babysitter for him and Dr.

Harley—the majority of which went to rent, transportation, and food, not savings.

At first, I primarily supported Dr. Myers, who also was hearing impaired, but after he left for a loftier position at the University of Minnesota, Dr. Harley took over AASP, and I became her right hand. Under her leadership, I gained even more responsibilities and was no longer tied to the desk. In my spare time, I completely overhauled the unused book collection in the office, and I created newsletters that promoted the program, including the faculty and special topics courses, like Black Women and Work.

Carla was one of Dr. Harley's many campus girlfriends who stopped by LeFrak Hall regularly. Some were faculty, like Dr. Mary Helen Washington in the English department. Others had titles like "department chair" or dean. I called Carla "Dr. Gary" or "Dean Gary" just to be on the safe side. In actuality, she was neither. Carla was an attorney by training, and she was an Associate Director for the Office of Minority Graduate Affairs, which, like the McNair Program, helped underrepresented students access and persist in graduate school.

I paused from my work and started to recite my tale of owing money, getting kicked out of school, and working to save so that I could go back to Howard University, but Carla cut me off.

"You need to be in school. You need to be in school," she insisted. "You are too smart to be sitting here without a degree. Why don't you transfer here?"

Up until this point, I had not given serious thought to transferring to another school, especially not the University of Maryland. Howard University was my home. In fact, I currently was living in D.C. within a small radius of the campus, renting a micro bedroom in LeDroit Park with two current Howard students. Although I wasn't in school, I wanted to be near it, *needed* to be near it. From time to time, I would hang out with Lalania and go to campus events like Homecoming and the Boyz II Men concert trying to catch a contact high of sorts and pass like I was a real student. I was a hard worker, and I was highly motivated, dammit. I *deserved* to be in school. Besides, I couldn't think of anything else I would do or any place where I would be besides college.

The University of Maryland was just a regular, big, white state school and not at all special like my beloved HU. I wasn't fazed by the black, red, gold, and white school colors. The marching band was boring. Heavy D didn't just pop by on campus during his time off. I had tasted the good life at Howard, and I couldn't fathom settling for less.

But time was moving on.

My appeal letter to Howard University president Franklyn Jenifer, sent along with a cover letter from a HBCU graduate, attorney Roberta Wright, who was a part-time lecturer for AASP, went unanswered. I started receiving graduation announcements from Lalania, Mellonie, Rhonda, and Nicole, all of my closest friends from Howard. Lalania had received a job offer from Eli Lilly Pharmaceutical Company—a whole $40,000 a year salary—and I was making minimum wage as an administrative assistant. Sean "Puffy" Combs started his own label, Bad Boy Records after being fired from Uptown Records. Everyone was advancing, and I was not, and my formula was not working.

Meanwhile, Rob and I were on parallel tracks. Freshly back from the Persian Gulf, Rob proposed to me in front of Park Square residence hall, where Lalania lived, on the same night that Dwayne Wayne proposed to Whitley Gilbert at the airport. We agreed that it was more like a promise engagement. The proper order was: finish school, get married, and get good jobs. But Rob was shocked to learn that he did not qualify for school benefits after all (because he "signed the wrong paperwork," according to the Marine Corps recruiter). He started working as a bank teller counting bills by hand.

Getting back in school seemed less and less probable for either of us, so Rob and I started planning our wedding. Maybe I could keep working in the Afro American Studies Program, take a few classes here and there, and someday become office manager, I calculated.

After a year of working full-time there, I had come to know the University of Maryland area very well. I knew the ins and outs of McKeldin Library because I sometimes had to check out books for Dr. Harley, plus I was on a first name basis with every Black senior administrator, plus I had gotten to know Jennifer, Jeanne, Tish, Craig, Seth, and other graduate students who either were Teaching Assistants or Research Assistants for the Program, plus I had a favorite apple cinnamon muffin that I would get regularly at South Campus Dining Hall, plus Len Bias lived and died there. And all of this was multiplied by the fact that I even had my own private office in the Afro American Studies Program where I hung posters of *School Daze* and the stars of *Boyz N The Hood* and had a bookshelf where I stored titles like *The Black Seminoles* and *Black Indians* that I was reading for fun.

Besides, the math made sense. Being a Maryland resident would greatly reduce my tuition and expenses and ultimately would be cheaper than attending Howard. I warmed up to the idea of transferring and approached Carla. She offered to write a memorandum to the Admissions Office asking them to review my transfer application with an unofficial transcript. I submitted my materials, held my breath, and waited.

I had no idea how I would pay off the debt to Howard University, if ever. My paycheck and even the babysitting money that I made all went to rent, transportation, and food. After 18 months of making $50 payments here and there, I had brought down my balance only by a small fraction.

The remainder was $1,100.

ON PAPER

Ronald E. McNair Postbaccalaureate Achievement Program
Through a grant competition, funds are awarded to institutions of higher education to prepare eligible participants for doctoral studies through involvement in research and other scholarly activities. Participants are from disadvantaged backgrounds and have demonstrated strong academic potential. Institutions work closely with participants as they complete their undergraduate requirements. Institutions encourage participants to enroll in graduate programs and then track their progress through to the successful completion of advanced degrees. The goal is to increase the attainment of Ph.D. degrees by students from underrepresented segments of society.
–U.S. Department of Education

"Professors are up to 25 times more likely to have a parent with a Ph.D." –Morgan et al (2022)

The Houppert Memorial Shakespeare Competition is named for Joseph W. Houppert, a beloved and tenured faculty member–in fact, a Shakespeare expert–in the University of Maryland's English Department. According to campus literature, Houppert exhibited great concern for the teaching of undergraduate students, and his faculty colleagues created the essay contest in his memory. The undergraduate winner each year receives a monetary prize, as well as public recognition during commencement. The Houppert contest epitomizes the crème de la crème of the department.

Mr. Houppert was no longer among the faculty by the time I transferred from Howard University. While at Howard, I toyed with the idea of majoring in political science, psychology, and African American Studies—not to mention all of the English classes that I aced as an Honors student. I figured that because reading and writing came naturally to me, I should go in a <u>different</u> direction. I thought that I needed to pick a major that was more challenging, something I had to stay up all night for. I came to college to elevate myself, after all, and I needed the blood, sweat, and tears to show for it. Why focus on subjects that I was already good at, I reasoned with myself.

By fall 1993, just one semester after transferring to the University of Maryland, I had gone all in with a new major: *English Language and Literature*—a good thing, too, since technically I was in my junior year. The clock was ticking, and I needed to graduate.

I often admired and grew close to my high school English teachers at T.C. Williams—all of them white—including Ms. Rebecca Buckbee, who had the unenviable task of teaching British literature to a bunch of know-it-all, hormone-filled teenagers. I was inspired by Ms. Buckbee, Mr. Ed Cannon, and Mr. Patrick Welsh, my 10th, 11th, and 12th grade English teachers, and I thought perhaps I would someday mold young minds in the classroom, just like they had mine. Majoring in English meant that I could continue to read a lot, and I heard that it was a great path to law school. Just in case.

I had received a fair amount of praise for my writing both in and out of school starting as early as first grade. In addition to those letters that I sent Mom while she was away in the Army, I also authored and illustrated my own short stories, including "The Kid and The Magic Lamp" about a young Black girl who befriends a genie. In 10th grade I won first place in the school's prose contest for a fictionalized story about my great aunt Phoebe's daughter Helen Rose who committed suicide by eating rat poison.

During freshman year at UNC Chapel Hill, I attempted bad poetry that was inspired by Nikki Giovanni and Langston Hughes. I also composed strongly worded letters to school newspapers about racial microaggressions that I uncovered. Declaring an English major was a chance for me to make it official and to declare how serious I was about writing and the power of the pen.

All University of Maryland English majors had to have a concentration, and I, despite my home library filled with Black authors and my attempts to write in a modern Black tradition, decided on British literature. It was pretty clear that "real" English majors studied Brit Lit and mastered Shakespeare, in particular. *Dead Poets Society* and movies like it taught us that humanities were the domain of quirky, privileged white guys who stood on chairs during class, quoted the Bard, and spoke Latin phrases to their young charges.

One of the first English faculty I encountered at the University of Maryland was Kent Cartwright, a truly inspiring teacher who wore a necktie and dark blazers to class, was far from stuffy, pretentious, or eccentric. He told jokes often at his own expense and never seemed to take himself, or the material, *too* seriously.

In class, we focused heavily on *Writing with Style*—a wisp of a paperback book that laid a strong writing foundation for me. Going forward, I was hyper aware of split infinitives and made sure that I had "active" verbs in my sentences whenever possible.

"Don't bury the lede!" Prof. Cartwright would exude as he moved from one side of the classroom to another. We could barely keep our eyes on him. "Put the meat of your idea at the beginning of your sentences. Make sure every paragraph has a topic sentence!" He called out to us as though we were an athletic team preparing for the national tournament game.

Cartwright also would dazzle us with his enthusiasm for Shakespeare. As a result, the material never felt out of reach in that class. Not only did I actually understand what I was reading, I even formed my own opinions about the plays.

As much as I admired Ms. Buckbee, I hated having to memorize a section from *Hamlet* and then recite the words in front of my mostly white peers who weren't paying any attention. I often was only one of a handful of Black students in

Honors English, a precursor to AP English with Mr. Welsh, and I just wanted to get through the material and get back to my seat as soon as possible. I rolled my eyes every time we discussed a/b/a/b rhyme patterns. *Who cares*, I murmured under my breath.

But under Cartwright's tutelage, I realized that I cared. There were feminist themes to explore and quirky plays I had never heard of before, not just the usual canon of *Macbeth*, *Othello*, and *Romeo and Juliet*. Keenly aware that he had a new Shakespeare convert in his hands, Prof. Cartwright encouraged me to submit an essay for the Houppert contest that spring.

"You've got a great feel for the material. Go on," he winked and smiled brightly.

That spring semester, I willingly enrolled in another Shakespeare course, along with an upper-division seminar on John Dryden, William Congreve, and Aphra Behn, proving to myself and others that I could master European literature. I would earn As in these classes, too. All of these wins—high marks, praise from white professors who were experts in their field, and the McNair Scholars Program—signaled to me that I was graduate school ready, and I wanted to be a Shakespeare scholar I decided.

With shaky hands, I pulled out a floppy disc, took a deep breath, and selected my final essay from Professor Cartwright's class—an enthusiastic analysis of *Love's Labour's Lost*. I received an A on that paper, a difficult feat already. I figured that with Cartwright's blessings and comments in the margins, I could make revisions that were Houppert worthy.

A few months later, I received a letter in the mail with my fate. It was on quality cream letterhead direct from the English department. Probably Classic Laid, most likely 24lb. Mom, who had started a company that provided administrative support to small businesses, had taught me how to identify different grades of professional paper.

"All paper is not the same," she explained. In fact, she taught me that lesson early in life when I watched her wrap Christmas gifts every year. No matter how hard times were, thin, nondescript wrapping paper—the kind you get from Peoples Drugstore or a clearance section—was verboten. Only the uncouth used it, and we were never to stoop that low.

I knew that paper types reinforce any message sent. The weight, brightness, texture, and opacity of paper all conveyed different meanings. Multipurpose paper was for *common* use. This letter was on the good stuff.

> "I am delighted to inform that you have won the award for the best undergraduate essay on Shakespeare . . . The Houppert Committee congratulates you on your accomplishment and extends its best wishes for your future literary studies . . . It was a delight to read a sensible and interesting paper on *Love's Labor's Lost.*"

The letter was signed by Sandy Mack of the Houppert Committee.

With tears in my eyes, I gasped, being careful not to get the paper wet. I had to make sure that it remained in excellent condition when I showed it to Mom.

Maynard "Sandy" Mack, Jr. was another Shakespeare scholar in the department. He had been teaching at the university for 20 years and was actively involved in the University Honors program, as well as Undergraduate Studies. He earned his undergraduate degree and doctorate in English at Yale University. Sandy's father, Maynard Mack, Sr., also was a Shakespearean scholar. The elder taught at Yale for 45 years; and in 1996, an endowed professorship was named in his honor. Mack, Sr. received his undergraduate and graduate degrees from Yale, and <u>his</u> father (Sandy's grandfather) was an English professor, as well. Sandy's sister, Sara, earned her doctorate from Harvard and would become professor emerita of classics at UNC-Chapel Hill.

I didn't know any of this history when I decided to visit Sandy's office hours after I received notice about my award. I just knew that Mack was a member of the selection committee and that he had validated my newfound professional goal. Not only would I go to graduate school, but I would also become a professor! I had a <u>future</u> in literary studies, according to Sandy. I held tight to that letter as though it were a passport.

I didn't have a script prepared when I appeared before Professor Mack's open door, and I wasn't exactly sure what I would ask. As a participant in the McNair Program back at Howard University, I had been coached on how to perform undergraduate research with minimal direct supervision.

My cohort mates and I had taken personality assessments, and I knew that I was an ENFP, according to Myers Briggs. Somehow knowing our personality type would help us succeed in graduate school, although we weren't sure how. We had begrudgingly worn navy blue and black business casual clothes in the hot muggy D.C. summer and visited places like the Brookings Institute where we learned about research-based careers.

These were the activities and behaviors of pre-graduate students, as they were taught to me. I merely was following the playbook for a first-generation student of color, and at this moment, I was in a familiar position and self-assured. I had prior experience successfully reaching out to faculty, so my confidence was high.

❊ ❊ ❊

Two years prior, I had knocked on a different professor's door in eager anticipation. I was still a Howard student and was participating in a six-week McNair summer research program, which is required of all Scholars. At this time, I was obsessed with media criticism, film, in particular. It was the early 1990s, and there was a renaissance of Black filmmakers thanks to the likes of Spike Lee, Matty Rich, and John Singleton, whose directorial debut, *Boyz N The Hood*, released in 1991.

About 20 of us McNair Scholars from various local institutions resided at American University for the program's duration. We didn't have a lot of guidance or parameters besides 1) take a summer statistics class on campus and 2) serve as an apprentice for a professor's research. This was standard practice among McNair summer intensives, i.e., get a basic grasp of stats and shadow a faculty member to learn the ropes of academia. The pathway to going to graduate school was via apprenticeship, regardless of your discipline. We had to identify a faculty mentor on our own, hoping to find a good match based on mutual interests. Be seen, not heard, and collect a stipend the likes of which most of us had never received in one check before.

Much to my roommate Bridget's annoyance, I regularly stayed up until two in the morning reading whatever books I could get my hands on. By the second week, I skipped the statistics class altogether—further annoying Bridget—since I rationalized that I wasn't a quantitative researcher, anyway. I was one of few people interest in the arts in the summer research program, and the program director, a Black female graduate student in social work, wasn't sure what to do with me, anyway. What kind of "research" does an arts and humanities student do?

My initial goal for the summer was to offer my services to a new Black film journal whose headquarters was in the D.C.

area. I went to their office one time but they also seemed uncertain what to do with a scrappy undergraduate student, even if they didn't have to pay for her services. Undeterred, I took the Metro bus across town back to my home campus and literally walked the empty halls of the Howard University Department of Communications in search of an opportunity.

I stopped in front of an open doorway. There sat a man who looked to be in his 40s or 50s with skin the color of dark milk chocolate. He reminded me of Mr. Stanley from UNC Chapel Hill or one of my great uncles back in North Carolina. Amidst the clutter within the office were knickknacks and other memorabilia from Ethiopia. From where I stood, I could see piles of papers and manila folders all over his desk.

He looked up from his work.

"May I help you?"

I couldn't place his accent specifically, but my ear did pick up the African intonations.

"Uhh, do you need any help?"

I gushed that I loved films but I wanted to *study* them, not make them. I took a breath and explained that I had to complete a research project within six weeks and—best of all—he didn't have to pay me. We always mentioned our "free" labor to incentivize faculty mentors and sponsors.

Not one to look a gift horse in the mouth, apparently, the gentleman waved me in further.

"I'm Abiyi," he said and motioned for me to sit down. His enthusiasm matched mine when he described the project that he was working on. Abiyi explained that he was studying not just Black films themselves but how journalists and movie critics—most of them white—wrote about them. In their reviews, did the writers address the content of the films, including aesthetic choices, like cinematography? Or was the focus on how audiences reacted to the film or how close the subject matter was to "reality"? In a nutshell, Abiyi argued that Black filmmakers were treated differently than their white counterparts, their work often tied to realism and "authenticity," which undermined their artistry and creative licenses.

He needed help surveying movie reviews from major newspaper outlets around the country like *The New York Times*. I would later learn that this was coding. Ford said that the work was not sexy but I would be helping him complete the dissertation that he was working on. I had never heard of "research" like this before. I had written several papers, of course. But my McNair colleagues were getting involved in laboratories or inputting data into spreadsheets.

"Are you interested, *La'*Tonya?"

He said my name like my mom does, with an emphasis on the "La."

I had only a vague idea what a dissertation was— a really long paper it sounded like—but I shook his hand in agreement happy to finally be on track with the summer program.

What he didn't tell me that day is that Abraham Abiyi Ford founded Howard University's film program, co-founded the

School of Communications, and is the founding chair of the former Department of Radio, Television and Film in 1971, one year after I was born. By 1982, the MFA in Film Program, the only graduate film program at an HBCU, also was established under his direction. Professor Ford earned an associate's degree from Piney Woods Junior College in Mississippi before transferring to Columbia University where he earned both a bachelor's degree and a MFA. Despite all of these professional accomplishments, here he was completing his doctorate in African Studies at Howard.

Like Sandy Mack, Abiyi Ford descended from a family of educators. In response to Marcus Garvey's return to Africa movement in the late 1920s, Ford's parents, native to Barbados, relocated to Ethiopia, which is where Abiyi and his brother were born. His father, Rabbi Arnold Josiah Ford, was Garvey's musical director and his mother, Mignon Lorraine Innis, founded Princess Zennebe Worq High School, the first secondary school for girls and the first modern co-educational school in the country.

I knew nothing of Abiyi's backstory during those six weeks. At the time, he just seemed like a friendly, albeit busy older student who needed some help while he was finishing up a dissertation chapter. My primary task was to use microfilm to read reviews of *Juice, Straight Out of Brooklyn*, and *Boyz N The Hood* and to take notes on what I found. Although I wasn't sure how, Abiyi swore I was helpful and regularly expressed his gratitude.

I figured, if graduate school was anything like those six weeks, surely, I could hack it. I imagined a future of more late nights reading library books and dutifully taking handwritten notes on a legal pad, which denoted <u>serious</u> study.

That was two years prior, and in Sandy Mack's office, I expressed enthusiasm for my new passion, Shakespeare. The official award letter was folded neatly in a notebook that was buried deep in my backpack.

"I'm La'Tonya," I announced, as though he was expecting my arrival. When Sandy paused, I clarified. "I won the Shakespeare essay contest? And I wanted to speak with you about going to graduate school. I'm really excited about going, and I want to focus on race and possibly gender, too. But I don't know what schools I should apply to, and since you are an expert, I thought I would ask you."

If Sandy flinched, I didn't notice. He remained seated and kept smiling.

"I see."

I could tell that he was choosing his words carefully.

"Well, are you surrrrre that you want to go to graduate school? Getting a Ph.D. takes a lot of *hard work*."

He kept smiling.

I nodded.

"Yes, I am sure."

"Well. It is true that your essay won," he confirmed and then paused as though weighing something over in his mind. "But I must say, the competition was not as good this year."

Sandy shared this information as though it were a gift to me. His tone was light, almost conspiratorial like he was letting me in on a secret—one that I should be grateful for—and going forward we would be pals. My win, he implied, was an aberration, a fluke, an asterisk on the historical roster of past Houppert winners because my essay, although shitty, was less shitty than the other shitty submissions.

In that moment and in a matter of seconds, I could feel my spirit rise from my physical body and hover above the room, as though I was watching the encounter happen to someone else.

That poor girl. What a dummy.

I was confused. After all, I was an Honors student and a McNair Scholar. According to Myers Briggs, an ideal career for me was college professor. I earned a 3.7 cumulative GPA and had nearly a 4.0 in advanced literature courses. I had already been a research assistant helping a kind graduate student finish his dissertation at Howard University. By this time, even as a transfer student, I was the lead research assistant on a book project helmed by award-winning historian Sharon Harley, and I was supervising a research team, including doctoral students. I had won an essay contest sponsored by *The Washington Post* about the importance of Black and Latino coalition building in the D.C. area. I had interned for Congresswoman Eleanor

Holmes Norton on Capitol Hill the semester that I thought I wanted to work in public policy.

I had served as an undergraduate teaching assistant, and while my GRE verbal scores were just okay, I only got two questions wrong on the entire GRE analytical section—the old school one with the logic problems. I accomplished all of these things while working 20-30 hours a week at AASP and also commuting to campus via public transportation, regularly studying on the bus and the Metro train.

On paper, I was a model graduate school applicant.

Despite the encouraging words he wrote in that award letter, Sandy took one look at me, asked no questions, and decided that I was not prepared to walk through the same gate as him, his father, and his father's father.

I thanked him for his time and on shaky legs, I left Sandy Mack's office and found myself crying in the hallway of the English department. Surrounding me on both sides were bulletin boards filled with colorful 11x17 high gloss flyers about Study Abroad in England, GRE Prep courses, and M.A. and Ph.D. programs all over the country and the world.

I'm not sure how I got there, but at some point, I looked up and saw a young professor in her office in the same corridor. I had heard of Dr. King, one of the new professors in the department. Word tended to spread quickly whenever there was a new Black faculty member, and it seemed like Dr. Harley was friends with all of them and was keeping tabs, like the big sister within a sorority.

Nicole had a kind smile, a gentle voice, and a beautiful head of thick black hair. She was young and quite stylish and reminded me of Freddie Brooks on "A Different World." I had never seen a professor like her before.

"Are you OK?" she called out when she realized that I clearly was not. "Come in. What's wrong??"

I took small steps toward a seat next to her and, unable to hold back, I recounted the conversation with Sandy moments before.

Nicole's face was grim but her eyes remained soft and sympathetic.

"You absolutely should apply for graduate school," she said firmly. The only thing she knew about me was the story I just shared with her.

Professor King had recently completed her doctorate at the University of Pennsylvania with a focus on Caribbean literature. She told me about her friends Kim F. Hall and Arthur L. Little, both Black, who were experts in a field I had never heard of before: race and Early Modern Studies. I turned those words over and over in my mind feeling like puzzle pieces were coming together, wondering if they fit. If I wanted to continue down this path, then I definitely should have UPenn on my list, Nicole advised me. That was <u>the</u> place to train if I wanted to specialize in this area.

With that bit of guidance about the graduate school admissions process—more than I had received until that point—I left Professor King's office a bit more assured than I had felt

20 minutes prior. But then I had a new concern: *Was I Ivy League material*? Sandy's comments lingered in my head creating doubts that hadn't existed before.

Although my dreams were temporarily shattered, I did have clearer direction now thanks to Nicole. I could not and did not tell anyone else what transpired between Sandy and me. I was embarrassed and just wanted to put it out of my mind.

"LT!"

Dr. Harley called out to me one day a few weeks later. I jumped out of my seat and trotted into her office running through my head any phone message I may have forgotten to give her or a memorandum I forgot to draft. By this time, she was chair of the Afro American Studies Program.

"Why didn't you tell me about what happened with that white professor in the English department? What's his name again??"

She scrunched up her face like she smelled something bad, her auburn hair gleaming in the sunlight.

"You mean Dr. Mack?"

I was stunned, as I wondered how she possibly found out.

She waved her hand in disgust.

"Yes, Sandy something or other. That man has some *nerve*. Who does he think he is?"

She was incensed and her cheeks were a little pinker than usual. Her voice kept going up in octaves. Again, she demanded to know why I didn't tell her and why she had to find out from Nicole King.

Unbeknownst to me, Dr. King told Dr. Harley and other Black women faculty about my interaction with Sandy Mack. Dr. Harley, along with feminist sociologist Bonnie Thornton Dill and my mentor, the incomparable Mary Helen Washington, founded an informal faculty support group two years prior in 1992. They called themselves Sister Scholars and were established to build community among Black female professors.

By 1996, the group would expand beyond the University of Maryland campus to include scholars from various local institutions, such as American University, George Mason University, Coppin State University, and the Smithsonian Museum, not unlike my McNair Program. Later known as the Black Women and Work Research Seminar or the Black Women and Work Collective, the community would go on to receive a $250,000 grant from the Ford Foundation so that these women could present works in progress to one another and exchange ideas. In 2002, the group would publish an anthology, *Sister Circle: Black Women and Work*.

But in these early days, the Sister Scholars met more informally over dinner once a month. Members delighted in one another's accomplishments and soothed each other's wounds when dealing with disrespectful white and male colleagues.

Truthfully, I was hoping to put the entire incident behind me. Besides, Mack was a professor, and I was a student. What could be done?

But the Sisters were not having it. Via letter, the group confronted Sandy and demanded that he apologize for his racial microaggressions. They made it crystal clear that his behavior and words to me were unacceptable and that they were prepared to bring the incident to the dean of humanities should he not respond appropriately. Sandy complied. Eventually he sent a brief handwritten apology to me via campus mail to the Afro American Studies Program where I worked. He was sorry, didn't mean any harm.

That spring, Professor Cartwright cheered for me as I shook the hand of the department chair when I received my $100 Houppert Award prize at a departmental ceremony. After I completed my doctorate over ten years later, I emailed Dr. Cartwright to let him know the good news. He was as enthusiastic as ever.

"Not surprised," he wrote back. I would never hear from Sandy Mack again.

❊ ❊ ❊

Although I had committed to earning a Ph.D. and becoming a faculty member, as a McNair Scholar, I really had no idea what academia was like. My frame of reference mostly came from movies and in those films the students and faculty were all white. About graduate school, I knew even less. Absolutely no one in my family had ever made it that far. I thought that grad school would be like undergrad but on steroids—kind of like an academic camp where you just read and write *a lot more.*

The McNair Program prepared me for the logistical side of things, but not the political and definitely not the social. We Scholars thought that we just needed to work extra hard and to keep our grades up, have strong letters of recommendation, and write a compelling personal statement—a clear pathway toward success. Nowhere in our education were we prepared to combat the Sandy Macks of the world. My perseverance, note taking, undergraduate research experience, and high GPA simply were no match for someone whose grandfather was an English professor. My grandfather delivered mail for a living. It was not a fair fight.

Kent Cartwright, Abiyi Ford, Nicole King, and all of the Sister Scholars showed me the importance of mentorship. Each of them welcomed me into the academy in their own ways— Cartwright with enthusiasm, Ford with humility and grace, King and the Scholars with advocacy, conviction, and fire. I didn't know it at that time, but I came to realize the value of having a collective who has your back far beyond getting into graduate school.

That fall, under the guidance of Nicole King, Dr. Harley, and Dr. Mary Helen Washington, I applied to three doctoral programs: New York University, UCLA, and the University of Pennsylvania.

My acceptance letter from UPenn arrived in the mail on regular copy paper.

UNDOCUMENTED

The knock at the front door was sharp and urgent, like rapid-fire echoes reverberating through the house.

"Get away from that door! And move from that window!

Grandma's voice was sharp—unusually so, one of the few times she ever raised her voice at me. That's how I knew this visitor was unwelcome.

From my hiding spot, I peeked out anyway. The Insurance Man stood there, tall, light-haired, and polite, carrying his worn, leather bag filled with papers. He looked harmless to me. On previous visits, when he smiled and called Grandma "Mrs. Wise," it felt sincere, like he respected her in a way the rest of the world outside didn't.

I could see the older neighborhood boys racing each other on their ten-speed bikes, and the Amtrak train gave the house a gentle shake as it rumbled by.

But Grandma didn't open the door.

Sometimes, The Insurance Man would call on the phone before his arrival.

"She's not able to come to the phone right now," I would lie, my fingers crossed. I didn't understand insurance, but I understood avoidance. I learned early that if you couldn't pay, you stayed out of sight or got the hell out of Dodge.

❊ ❊ ❊

Now, as I stood inches from graduating from the University of Maryland, that memory felt sharp, like one of those knocks. The fear of being discovered—of someone calling me out—gnawed at my insides. I had been admitted to the university with an unofficial transcript from Howard University, and I never submitted the real thing. Once the gate was lifted, thanks to Carla Gary's memorandum vouching for me as a prospective transfer student, I ran to the other side and never looked back. I wasn't sure how I'd managed to cross the border into this academic world, but I knew it wasn't through the front door.

They could take it all away—the Houppert Award, my quest to a Ph.D. program.

All my work, erased.

I hadn't even realized I needed to *apply* to graduate. Who knew? It was just another invisible rule I'd stumbled upon. I read and re-read the University Bulletin—my chest tight and my breath shallow—and noted that an academic advisor had to review my paperwork and confirm that I was eligible to graduate. I had never been to an advisor before.

After first fleeing the U.S. for Canada, he landed in an inconspicuous neighborhood in Orange County, California–about 45 minutes outside of Los Angeles. It was hot and far away from Alexandria. Perfect.

Going by the name of Rudy Santiaga, he ingratiated himself in a largely Spanish-speaking community. To improve his fluency, he took Spanish language classes at Mission Viejo Community College and the University of Southern California.

A few decades later, Jerry was arrested for his crimes in Northern Virginia and served a number of years. Again. He has a few theories about who dropped the dime.

※ ※ ※

My uncle Dale had planned to go to college just not right after high school. He wanted to get out of Alexandria and see the world. Knowing that his dad (a Navy guy), his brother Ronnie (Army), and his sister and my mother, Gloria (also Army) among other family members all benefitted, he decided to enlist and expand his opportunities. And he did get to travel–going all the way to Germany and back.

He returned to the D.C. area at the tender age of 23 looking for his next adventure, including, hopefully, college. But my grandfather wasn't in on the plan. Granddaddy spent what little college savings he had set aside for Dale.

"You made your choice," he said wryly perhaps believing that his son only had one shot at higher education. Dale was on his own.

A self-professed tech geek, Dale spent a good amount of his time tinkering with computers and other gadgets—often taking things apart and rebuilding them from scratch. He only need to watch someone do it one time. Oftentimes, he just figured things out on his own. Unc started taking a few computer classes at nearby Northern Virginia Community College to brush up on his skills.

At one point, he fast-talked himself into a help desk position at a company. When the interviewer started tossing around a bunch of computer languages—A+, JavaScript, and Python—Dale flashed him a smile and nodded along. His charm is another one of his strong qualities.

"Yep, got it," he grinned.

He had no idea what this man was talking about.

Unc enrolled at George Mason University part-time to take more advanced computer classes. He was just one step ahead at work. Anytime someone asked him to do something he hadn't gotten to in class, Dale would calmly defer and say, "Why don't I just watch you first?" And then he got it on the first try.

❉ ❉ ❉

Taking Classes

My cousin William is two years older than me but the youngest of eight in his household. His mother bribed him with a car to keep him from going to college. She just didn't see the point.

Brother number two, a gymnast, had managed to successfully navigate the guidance counseling minefield at T.C. Williams High School and attended UPenn where he studied theater.

While it was known that he was "different," no one ever talked about it openly, and then he went off to college and rarely came home. The family saw pictures of him with other men and they seemed "different," too. Clearly, college was to blame, according to their mother.

It didn't help matters when Harry, the seventh child, buckled under the pressure of attending the College of William & Mary, studying math because people told him that he should. The anxiety became too much and Harry returned to Alexandria after two years. This was more evidence for William's mom that college was of the devil and not the place to be. Will should set his sights on a good government job instead. A shiny, burgundy Cadillac would ensure that he got to work on time.

For most of high school, William intended to play football at one of three universities: Nebraska, Tennessee, or Oklahoma hoping to fit in as a running back in their wishbone offense. But then his knee started acting up and he was told, just like Boobie Miles in *Friday Night Lights*, that he would need career-ending knee surgery.

After graduating from T.C. Williams, William first parked cars at the Ramada Inn in Old Town and then transitioned over to George Mason University, working in campus information. He was advised to enroll in a few classes there since they were free after all to state employees. A "C" average student in high school, Will realized that getting good grades actually wasn't too difficult for him in college. He took random classes at first but then homed in, studying music with the goal of being a producer. Eventually, he switched to the Continuing Education program.

Now a part-time student and a full-time employee, William started attending campus events, going to Que parties, and eventually joined Phi Beta Sigma International Fraternity, Inc. He and I would meet up on campus, and occasionally he would visit me at Howard University. Caught in the middle, he didn't tell his mom about these classes, and he also didn't tell many people at George Mason that he was not a full-time student. You either were in college or not.

The guys he was hanging out with at the Chapter II nightclub—those who were driving Maximas with spoiler kits and spinning on 20-inch rims—started calling him "Joe College" and showing up at George Mason parties to pull the numbers of all the pretty girls.

After about one year, Will enrolled at the Computer Learning Center and then Strayer College, where he earned a certificate. With the support of his fiancée, he started networking classes on a regular basis. Marriage looming and looking toward the future, Will wanted to have a career and not just a job. He turned to the University of Atlanta, a private, for-profit distance education school originally based in Birmingham, Alabama. They promised him that they would take all of his prior experience into consideration and that his four-year degree would be accelerated. But then the added requirements started to add up. Will realized that he would be in school for another two years.[1]

Three or four more years passed. As he was thinking about reviving his educational journey, Will called Strayer to request a copy of his transcript and learned that he had successfully completed his A.A. degree.

He had no idea.

He was just taking classes.

---

[1] Founded as Barrington University in the 1990s, this institution has a history of fraudulent claims, including a chairman who falsely claimed having a master's and doctorate degree and accreditation that it did not have. The school stopped enrolling students in 2012. William didn't know about any of these claims at the time.

CLOSE READING

It always seemed like Mary Helen Washington was happy to see me when I stopped by her office, and this day seemed no different. Before enrolling in one of her upper division seminars, most of my previous encounters with her were at a respectful distance. I knew that she was one of the Sister Scholars who spent quality time with Dr. Sharon Harley and other Black women professors and administrators. And I heard that she was a foremost authority on African American literature. In fact, there were paperback copies of her work in the Afro American Studies Program office. It was hard for me to reconcile that the person's name on the cover of *Invented Lives: Narratives of Black Women 1860-1960* and *Memory of Kin: Stories about Family by Black Writers* belonged to the same woman who came into the AASP office typically in shorts and sandals. To me, she was just Mary Helen, bright-eyed and wide-smiled with curly greying hair that she kept cutting shorter and shorter.

I couldn't wait to tell Mary Helen about a movie I recently had seen starring teenager Sean Nelson, along with

Giancarlo Esposito and Samuel L. Jackson—the latter two who also appeared in Spike Lee's *School Daze*. Without stopping, I carried on about the chess symbolism in the film. I was so proud of myself for picking up on these themes and imagery, which would have flown over my head before now.

I worked so hard in Mary Helen's upper division African American literature course to earn even a B+. It seemed like my analyses were only skimming the surface, and she kept challenging me to consider word placement, theme, and imagery. I had never been pushed so hard before, not even in Professor Cartwright's Shakespeare class. The turning point came when I received—finally!—an A on a close reading that I submitted on a passage from Albert Murray's vastly underrated novel, *Train Whistle Guitar*. I was starting to feel like a real English major now.

Mary Helen waited for me to finish my enthusiastic film review. After a pause, she looked at me over the top of her eyeglasses and said, "La'Tonya, that movie was shitty."

I was stunned and temporarily muted. Here I was practically kneeling and submitting a literary offering to the high priestess, and it was rejected. What about the chess pieces, I thought to myself. I didn't dare challenge her wisdom out loud.

With the calmness of a preschool teacher, Mary Helen countered my take on this movie. She pointed out how the main character, a Black 12-year-old boy, was without a community, and he was acting alone in a world of adults. Did that seem right to me? Who was he connected to, Mary Helen asked, looking at me directly through those glasses. She went on to mention the pervasive racial stereotyping of the Black and Latino characters, and on top of it all, Nicole, played by N'Bushe Wright, had no agency whatsoever. She was, to use the chess imagery, just a pawn in this narrative about hypermasculinity. Who cares about all of the symbolism when the content was trash? My job as a literary critic wasn't simply to point out all of the tools that a writer (or filmmaker) used but to step back and think about how the whole house came together. And as a Black woman, I needed to call out racism and sexism when I saw it and to think more deeply about the impact of an artistic work. Did these images actually ring true?

I was momentarily deflated. How did I not see that the movie was shitty? I realized that I had so much more to learn as I was approaching graduate school.

Mary Helen refused to let me or any student call her "Dr. Washington." Meanwhile I would never <u>ever</u> consider calling Dr. Harley by her first name. A native Washingtonian, Sharon Harley earned her B.A. in history from Saint Mary-of-the-Woods College in Indiana the same year that Mom gave birth to me as a high school junior. She had a twin sister named Sheila who, at this time, was starting a new career as an attorney at age 50. Their father was a dentist, and Sharon, Sheila, and their two brothers were raised in a middle-class community. Mary Helen came from a working-class background in Cleveland, Ohio and raised in what she once described as a fiercely Catholic and racially conservative family. In the late 1960s, she was the first Black graduate student in the history of the English department at the University of Detroit where she earned her doctorate. Together, Sharon Harley and Mary Helen Washington, two pioneering scholars, provided me a firm foundation in Black feminist theory in academia.

Having successfully applied for graduation without drawing attention to the fact that I had never submitted an official transcript when I was admitted to the University of Maryland, it was time to prepare for my next step.

"You should apply to UCLA," Mary Helen told me emphatically as I was considering graduate programs during my senior year. The one in Los Angeles? I was incredulous. I had done my fair share of California dreaming, but that was mostly about the magical land of Oakland, not Los Angeles, the land of fake tans and Hollywood. In fact, the notion seemed more unlikely than me attending an Ivy League school. While I had been fantasizing about moving to California since my junior high days when I thought I would be an editor for *Right On!* magazine, I never really imagined living there. The state was nearly 3,000 miles away from all of my family and friends who spanned the East Coast from Connecticut down to North Carolina. No one was living west of Raleigh-Durham.

I also heard in the news about earthquakes and drive bys. I had seen *Boyz N The Hood* and *Menace II Society* several times, and I felt like an expert in South Central Los Angeles gangs: Crips wore blue; Bloods wore red. Avoid those colors at all costs.

That spring, my family and I were one of several million people who watched the LAPD chase O.J. Simpson across several highways in Southern California. Overall, it seemed like a dangerous place.

I wasn't convinced about UCLA's basketball prowess, either. I knew that the men's team had won several championships but that was forever ago during the 1960s and 70s. My family, including Grandma and my uncles, rooted for coach Pat Riley and the dominant Los Angeles Lakers. After all, James Worthy, a Gastonia, North Carolina native and former UNC Tar Heel, had been a star player on the team. As far as I was concerned, the best college basketball in the city was played near downtown Los Angeles over at the University of Southern California featuring twins Pam and Paula McGee, who I followed in *Jet* magazine, and, of course, Cheryl Miller, the greatest woman to ever hoop. But the UCLA Bruins in the 1980s and 1990s? I wasn't so sure.

Mary Helen was adamant that I at least apply to UCLA, and she coached me on the personal statement that I submitted there, along with UPenn, Rutgers University's M.A. program, and New York University. To help me prepare, she asked me several questions about my upbringing and my educational journey—and what role Mom played in any of it.

I thought back to all of the times that Mom confronted my teachers whenever they underestimated my abilities or attempted to pull me away from my best girlfriends in school. I recalled Mom telling me that I had to stick up for myself and then being a role model and showing me how to do it. I started thinking about her prized album collection that always traveled with us no matter how many apartments we lived in. She loved popular bands like Earth, Wind & Fire and The Ohio Players, but the albums that stood out to me the most were those by Chaka Khan and Millie Jackson, brown-skinned Black women with big hair and wide mouths, who were unapologetic about what they wanted.

Mom would get riled up about one particular song by jazz/R&B/soul songstress, brown-skinned Marlena Shaw. While she was cleaning the house on Saturdays, Mom sometimes would put on "Go Away Little Boy," which is part song, part rap, part stand-up comedy routine in a storytelling tradition of Shaw's contemporary, Millie Jackson. Mom would recite along with Marlena as she told the story of how she financially supported her partner who quit his job to open a "head shop" because he was tired of working for The Man.

"If I got to get up and go to work every day," Mom and Marlena said together, "every able body in the household supposed to go." If he is unable to meet those demands, then Marlena, with Mom as backup, crooned it was time to "go away, little boy" at the song's crescendo. But then, with the piano and trumpet keeping perfect time in the background all the while, the narrator eventually succumbs to the charms of her lover as he kisses her eyelids and promises that he will get a job by next Thursday. No matter how many times she played this song,

Mom would be irate at these turn of events in the narrative and blasted it as anti-feminist. I considered her view.

Marlena sure sounded pissed when she told the boy to "run, run, run, run, run, run, run" away. I noted that the music keeps its steady pace, yet Marlena's delivery shifts, signaling her emotions—starting fast and staccato, full of irritation at her 'lame man,' then turning smooth and sultry by the end, as she forgives him.

"But her voice sounds so pretty when she tells him he can stay," thinking about how Marlena's voice is in time with the twinkling piano at this point of the song. "So maybe," I hedged. "She didn't really want him to go after all," essentially calling Marlena's bluff.

Mom rolled her eyes.

"She gave in like a chump."

I just assumed that everyone talked to their parents about songs this way and, thanks to Mary Helen, came to realize that Mom had indeed given me permission to be a cultural critic, which is what I wrote in my personal statement for graduate school. Mary Helen also encouraged me to mention my working-class background and the fact that Mom had been an E5 sergeant in the Army and not a degree holding literature major herself. Through these conversations, I realized just how much Mom had shaped my views of popular culture by asking me to reflect on what I was reading, watching, or listening to and, like Mary Helen, she would let me know when something was shitty.

Since my run-in with Professor Sandy Mack, my interest in Shakespearean studies had started to wane. Mary Helen assured me that if I was serious about film criticism and if I wanted to write about movies like *Fresh* and other forms of popular culture, then I should explore Cinema Studies at New York University or cutting-edge English Departments, like the one at UCLA. I did so reluctantly hoping to stay within my comfort zone in the mid-Atlantic region. Getting a Ph.D. seemed like a big enough deal. Why add a cross-country move on top of it?

February 1995. I could hear the phone ring in Dr. Harley's office from where I sat at my administrative assistant's desk in an adjacent office.

"Yes, she's right here. . . LT!" I jumped. "Pick up the phone. It's for you."

"Hello?" I asked breathlessly.

"La'Tonyaaaaaa." It was Mary Helen on the other end. "I'm here at UCLA visiting Richard, and the selection committee just met." There was a pause. "You've been admitted!"

Richard Yarborough was a faculty member in the UCLA Department of English, a notable scholar of African American literature and culture and one of Mary Helen's closest friends. Apparently, he had been on the selection committee, and he gave Mary Helen the greenlight to share the good news with me. About a month later, I would receive a phone call from Valerie Smith, chair of graduate studies in the department, informing me in her husky voice about a diversity fellowship, known as Project 88, that I would receive which not only covered my tuition and fees but also provided me with a $14,000 annual stipend. I would be paid to go to school.

It was as if I had moved beyond the limits of long division, where debts were subtracted and remainders hung in the air. Now, I would step into a world of higher-order math—where instead of constantly dividing resources, I could be made whole. No longer forced to break down opportunities into fractions, I could once again think in terms of growth, multiplying possibilities in ways that had never felt possible before.

Grandma was less thrilled. She already was skeptical about me getting married to Rob at such a young age (22), and now I was talking about moving "halfway around the world." I knew that deep down she was happy about this opportunity for me, but her fear of the unknown—going to California—as well as the known—her own unhappy marriage—was palpable. There are perfectly good schools close by, like Georgetown. I was so smart, and she was certain that I would be admitted to any of them if I just applied.

"I don't know if I'll actually go, Grandma," I shrugged. It was a nice Hollywood fantasy, but I really thought of myself as an East Coast girl at heart—all baggy pants—one leg rolled up—high tops, and big coats. UPenn was only a two hour drive away and, not to mention, an Ivy League school. To me, attending a prestigious school like that was the ultimate payoff for years of hard work. I would be close to home, attend a fancy private school, and make my entire family proud.

I took an Amtrak train to Philadelphia for a three-day, two night admitted student excursion at UPenn, confidently navigating various modes of transportation from Southern Maryland. I arrived a little early before my host, a current graduate student, was at home, so I took a cab to the English department front office to say hello and to get my bearings. I walked into the office with my overnight bag in tow and introduced myself to the young woman at the front desk.

"Hi." I extended my hand to her. "I'm La'Tonya. I'm here for admitted students' day?"

Her face reddened.

"Oh! We weren't expecting you so - -" Then she stopped herself and shook her head. "Good to meet you." She told me her name. "It's just that . . . you're early!"

It was my turn to feel embarrassed.

"Uh . . . yeah. My host isn't home yet, and I wasn't sure where to go, so I came here. Hope that's ok?"

"No problem!" She said and gestured to a white student who was sitting nearby and called her name. "Can you show La'Tonya around? She's just been admitted to the doctoral program."

The student smiled, nodded, and rose from her seat. Just as she started to approach me, a Black student came in the office. She moved with purpose as though running an errand.

"No, wait!" The administrator called out. "You." She gestured to the unassuming Black student who was simply minding her business. "Can <u>you</u> show La'Tonya around?"

The student stopped in her tracks. "Uh, sure?" We looked at each other nervously both likely wondering what made her a better candidate to give me a campus tour while knowing full well what we had in common.

The visit went downhill after that.

The next day, a sunny, warm-for-March-day, I took a walking tour with other students of color who had been admitted to graduate programs throughout the university. I liked the city of Philadelphia, which I thought of as like an older sibling of Washington, D.C. All of the familiar colonial architecture and brick comforted me, like a home away from home. Mom and I sometimes would make the two or two and a half hour drive up to visit friends, and I always looked forward to getting a cheesesteak for the ride back. Nothing about Philly intimidated me.

My tour group gathered in a central quad area in front of an administration building. An enormous library took up almost an entire side of the area, but I felt at ease knowing that it was there. I didn't know what was inside those other buildings, but I knew that books resided in a library. A large sculpture of a broken white button right in front was endearing and gave me some flicker of hope.

My fellow admits were awestruck as we took off on foot in West Philadelphia. One guy, a Black man, gushed about how "lucky" and "grateful" he felt being admitted to Penn. Other students nodded in agreement. Those comments rubbed me the wrong way, and I couldn't help but roll my eyes. Sure, I was over the moon to be admitted to an Ivy League doctoral program but feeling grateful never entered my mind. Mom, Mary Helen, and Dr. Harley told me that I deserved to be there, as though there was no other decision for the selection committee to make. If anything, I felt like the department should be happy to have me. A cloud started to form over me, and I couldn't shake it.

After the walk, I attended lunch with other prospective students. The navy-blue tablecloth and linen napkins complimented the Penn Blue and Penn Red logos that were displayed everywhere. I felt like I was going on a blind date set up by a well-meaning friend, but there was no love connection.

Later in the day, I met Professor Kim Hall, my Shakespeare and race scholar hero, in her office—the same person that University of Maryland professor Nicole King told me to connect with. She asked me what other graduate programs I was considering. When I mentioned that I was choosing between Penn and UCLA, her face fell slightly then she chuckled. Kim sat forward a little and whispered, although we were the only ones in the small office, "If I were you, I'd go to UCLA."

These words calcified and started to confirm an intangible feeling that had settled in. I couldn't name it exactly, but my gut told me that Penn was not the place for me. The same places in West Philly that Mom and I had visited during our spur of the moment drives were some of the same places that current students told me were "dangerous" and to avoid. I could see myself living in the city, but not being a student there.

Rob decided to join me on the visit to UCLA. We arrived on a beautiful 70-degree day in the postcard perfect Westwood neighborhood where there were large movie theaters on the corner that showed only one movie. Somehow Rob figured out how to get to O.J. Simpson's house in Brentwood, but it was more plain and less impressive than it looked on the TV news.

The highlight of my trip included meeting Professor Arthur Little, Kim Hall's peer in Shakespeare and race studies. Thin and goateed with skin as smooth, dark, and shiny as ebony, he reminded me of R&B singer R. Kelly with a sophisticated vocabulary and wicked sense of humor. I also enjoyed my time chatting with a group of graduate students who happened to be on a break from class. They asked me about regular things like what TV shows I liked, not about "Ph.D." things—whatever those were. One of them was from Northern Virginia and had attended one of T.C. Williams's rivals. I could feel myself relax and started to wonder if this East Coast shorty could actually turn into a Cali girl.

On a Monday night in early April, the UCLA men's basketball team defeated the Arkansas Razorbacks to win its first championship title in 20 years. I took this as an omen, and my fate was sealed. I would not earn my doctorate at an Ivy League school. I was headed west to a national champion.

❖ ❖ ❖

My first test in graduate school was learning the different L.A. neighborhoods and freeways:
- Freeway numbers are referred to with "the" in front of them, e.g., the 10 or the 405, unlike 95 highway back home
- We lived south of the 10 freeway near USC in a place where most of my classmates never ventured and referred to as "South Central"
- Driving through our neighborhood felt like driving through the movie sets of not only *Boyz N the Hood* and *Menace II Society*, but especially *Devil in a Blue Dress* co-starring Denzel Washington and Don Cheadle as "Mouse," whose Texas accent I could hear in the voices of Black locals

When we first arrived in the fall, Rob and I crashed with Connie, a fellow Black graduate student in the department, for a few days until we found our rental home. Connie and I hit it off instantly, and we became inseparable. She lived on Slauson Avenue, not too far away from the neighborhood that we would call home for the next two years. Most importantly, Connie was from D.C. and reminded me of the best things about the East Coast. She was one year ahead of me in the program but two years younger than me in age. We were approximately the same height and were both born in July, only days apart. We spent so much time together that faculty and staff in the English department often confused us although we didn't look alike. I appreciated her casual style: her Doc Martin boots, her cropped hairstyle with a singular twist that fell over one eye, and her penchant for snorting while she laughed. Even I began to think of us as fraternal twins, although Connie already had a biological twin sibling. I was enthralled by her outlook on life and the casual way that she approached being in a doctoral program at UCLA, as though it were no big deal. We came from dissimilar educational backgrounds—her mother was a grade school teacher in Washington, D.C.—but in Connie I could see a version of me earning a Ph.D. If she could do it, then so could I.

From Connie I learned that we were part of a phenomenon called "Generation X," which I hadn't heard of before. She had recently read a novel of the same name written by Douglas Copeland and was marinating about whether or not this was simply a whitewashed concept. Leading up to the start of classes and even after the fall quarter began, Connie and I conducted our own independent research project renting a stack of movies from the hole in the wall video store across the street from her apartment: *Reality Bites*, *Tank Girl*, *Singles*, *Empire Records*, *If Lucy Fell*, *Before Sunset* and the like- many of which were set in Los Angeles and all considered Gen X texts. We enjoyed some of these movies and made fun of most of them. None of them really reflected our experiences as Black twentysomethings living in parts of the city that only appeared in the evening news or in 'hood movies.

We also studied L.A. culture in films about East Los Angeles, near downtown or a little farther east in Boyle Heights. At the time, Connie and I relied on public transportation to get around the city so we didn't get to this side of town too often. But thanks to *American Me*; *Blood In, Blood Out*; and *Mi Vida Loca*, we – naively– believed that we had some insight on Chicano culture and occasionally called each other "homes" and "ese."

When I checked in back home, I told Mom and Grandma about all of the places that I had seen in movies and on the news. Our one-bedroom home was only a few miles from the Magic Johnson movie theater on Crenshaw Boulevard. Rob and I drove our Ford Escort along the same path as Cher when she went retail therapy shopping in *Clueless*, and I even waved at the Electric Fountain as we rode by it in Beverly Hills, as though Cher–or someone–would wave back.

When Rob and I first arrived in L.A., I was determined to ride the city bus and walk to wherever I needed to go–just as I had back East–with my head down or my nose stuck in a book. Being mobile without relying on a car was a major part of my identity and reassured me that I was independent, capable, and competent. I learned another lesson–this time about Los Angeles sprawl and realized that it could easily take me 30 full minutes to travel ten miles. Reluctantly, I gave in and purchased a used electric blue Volkswagen Karmann Ghia that could only accommodate me and one other person.

One weekend Rob, Connie, and I went to the same diner featured in the movie *Swingers*—allegedly another Gen X film—and thought the food was overrated. And one Saturday I pulled over to the side of the road and called Rob from a pay phone when I realized that I was shopping at the same Nike store as Patricia Southall, former beauty queen and wife of comedian Martin Lawrence, star of *Bad Boys*, which was a major sleeper hit that year.

"I was, like, 20 feet away from her," I yelled into the phone. I started saying "yo!" and "son" less and less and began using "like" more and more as a filler during conversations. This was my new crazy life.

※ ※ ※

Classes finally began in late September. I didn't know what to expect from a graduate seminar. I had been in classes with less than 20 students at Howard University but was caught off guard by the setup in the UCLA English Department. For the most part, students sat at desks arranged in a circle or square all facing one another. Or we sat at large, conference-style wooden tables. There was no place to hide and no option to sit in the back row. I had to read at least one novel each week for every class I took, which often translated into three different books weekly—not to mention supplemental essays—which meant I was on track to read approximately 30 novels each term. I had to adjust to that pace, but the reading itself I could do. I struggled most with class participation. Not only were we supposed to read the material, but the professors also expected us to have original thoughts about it all —something that wasn't already obvious or written about.

Sheesh, I thought. *I'm barely getting through all of these novels, and you want me to have something <u>original</u> to say?*

During my first quarter, Professor Sonia Saldivar-Hull taught my favorite graduate seminar, which focused on Chicano literature, none of which I ever heard of before. The majority of my classmates were students of color, some of whom were two or three or more years ahead of me in the program. They were smart, dynamic, expressive, funny, and sure of themselves. I did not speak very often because I was too embarrassed to say something wrong. But to myself, I asked, *Who is Lacan? And what is the deal with this guy, Derrida, that people kept talking about?* Should I have known about them already? I wrote down their names, spelled them out phonetically, circled them in my notebook, and told myself to look them up later. I glanced around the room. Some people wrote furiously in leatherbound notebooks that easily cost $20 or more. Others wrote nothing at all—just listened intently and walked out of the room after it was over.

One day during class, my peers (me excluded) had a lively discussion about a novel written by Americo Paredes. I enjoyed it and could feel my mind expanding as I absorbed it and over the course of the term other novels by Sandra Cisneros, Ana Castillo, and new favorite, Helena Maria Viramontes.

One of my classmates started getting worked up over a particular passage.

"I was so excited when the dog grabbed the flag and ran away," he said, breathlessly, "because the flag symbolizes oppression and colonization."

Others nodded, so he kept going.

"And I just wanted to say, 'Run on, dog! You. run. on.'"

He swung his hand in the air for emphasis.

I sat back in my chair bewildered. Somehow, I missed all of this symbolism. I thought the dog was just ... a dog. In that moment and others that had come before it in this class and in others, I felt like maybe I was over my head with all of this Ph.D. stuff. If I couldn't do a basic close reading, maybe this wasn't for me, after all. A master's degree would be just fine. Mom and Grandma would be happy either way.

When I recounted the story later to Connie, who was not taking this class, she laughed and snorted at the same time.

"That's the dumbest thing I've ever heard," she said. "I bet he didn't even do the reading," which proved to be another lesson.

You can not do the reading?

Over time and by my second year in the program, with a lot of support from Connie and other grad students of color, I became more adept at grad seminar management. In a different seminar devoted entirely to Dutch philosopher, Søren Kierkegaard, the class once spent the entire three hours discussing one paragraph, and part of that time was devoted to one footnote only. By this point, I had learned the playbook, and I realized that I just needed to periodically make eye contact with the instructor and nod with confidence, as though I was following the discussion. I performed like I was paying attention. In reality, I wrote out grocery lists, and most of the time I made an alphabetical list of the 50 states and would follow that up with a list of their capitals. Keep writing, nod, make eye contact with whoever is speaking, go back to writing.

A turning point occurred during the winter quarter of my first year in the program. Winter is a notoriously tough term at UCLA. It's typically rainy at this time and most people just barely hang on until spring break. Here I sat on the second floor of Rolfe Hall located in North Campus. I was enrolled in a poetry class and on this day, we were discussing Yeats. Although it was February, it was a sunny and warm day, in the 80s, a lot like it was when I visited the campus as a prospective student. I stared out of the window, and when I returned my attention to the class, I watched my hand pick up a plastic bottle—something I rarely did back home in D.C. where we drank water from a cup or a glass.

Smart Girl: A First-Gen Origin Story

What was I doing? I started to ask myself. Was I making a difference? How dare I sit here reading poetry and *drinking from a water bottle* for goodness sake, while my entire family was back East most likely wearing long coats, gloves, and February appropriate winter boots. How could I sit here reading poetry of all things knowing that Granddaddy was carrying mail five days out of the week rain or shine?

Stupid, stupid girl, I thought.

One side of Rolfe Hall faced Campbell Hall, a three-story brick structure that looked like it had been built in the 1960s. I barely paid attention to this building when I was on campus, as I was laser focused on either the English Department or the research library. Connie and a few of the other graduate students of color encouraged me to apply for a tutoring job in Campbell Hall. Unbeknownst to me, inside was a student support program geared toward students of color and first-generation college students called the Academic Advancement Program, better known as AAP. If UNC Chapel Hill, Howard University, or the University of Maryland offered tutoring services, I wouldn't have known. I didn't engage in any campus support services, including tutoring, advising, or career counseling unless required to.

This looks like an urban high school was my first thought when I made my way over. AAP offices took up the entire first floor. In between the offices were large rooms filled with brown faux wood circular tables and plastic chairs. This is where tutoring took place. As I walked the hallways, I noted the plethora of fliers and photos printed from a color printer posted on bulletin boards like stamps in a collection book. The dusty hallway floors were black and white checkerboard patterned, and all of the office doors were reddish-brown wood. But what the area lacked in sophistication and the modern times, it made up for with charm. The energy was palpable. *So, this is where all of the people of color are*, I thought to myself.

I interviewed with an undergraduate student, Angelica, who would be my supervisor in the humanities lab. I noted that she pronounced her name "Ahn-hell-ee-ka," and she quickly corrected anyone who dared Anglicize it.

"You have to teach people how to say your name *correctly*," she said with a stern voice. "If I have to learn these white names, the least they can do is get mine right."

And with that, she tossed her long dark hair over one shoulder.

I didn't disagree and even felt a little intimidated by this 21-year-old.

AAP was founded in the 1970s. At the time, the program offered three main services: tutoring in most subjects, counseling, and mentoring. Eligible new students could also participate in a summer bridge program—one for new freshmen and one for new transfers. Tutoring was the crown jewel. In effect, it was student-led and student run. Tutors were those students who had successfully completed a course and with the recommendation of a faculty member would help current students taking the same course. Whenever possible, tutoring was done in groups and took place on the same day and time each week. Students had to sign up at the beginning of the term and not wait until they were struggling in a course. Tutors functioned more like facilitators, and it was their goal to empower the tutees to arrive at their own understanding. It was widely known that the smartest UCLA students proudly went to tutoring.

I was happy to see students who looked like me and who came from similar backgrounds. I began spending more time in Campbell Hall even when I wasn't on the clock. Occasionally, I would snag some leftover sandwiches and Diddy Riese cookies from an evening workshop that others left behind. And I got to know Mauricio, the custodian who was assigned to the building.

"Como estas?" he would ask me each evening as he pushed his cart from room to room.

"Bien," I would reply almost to myself as I was trying out this new language.

Thanks to Angelica, my first tutoring assignment was an Intro to Chicano Literature course that Professor Saldivar-Hull taught for undergraduates.

I rapped on the door and poked my head into Angelica's office.

"Hey," I said tentatively, holding the assignment in my hand. "I have my tutoring assignment. Are you sure? I mean, I only took that one class, and I don't really know any Spanish . . ." I trailed off.

"Yup." She said quickly and with a smile. "Remember, you aren't there to teach. Just get them to believe in themselves."

I nodded and walked away, not feeling at all as confident as Angelica was sounding.

As instructed, I visited Professor Saldivar-Hull's lecture, where I stood in front of the classroom and introduced myself during the first week of the spring term. I told the room of 75+ students the day and time that the tutoring session met. Dr. Saldivar-Hull gave me a little thumbs up as I scooted out of the room.

On the first day of tutoring, I got to Campbell Hall a little early. I found a table—not too big—and wrote my name, the table number, and the name of the course on the whiteboard and waited. In came Danny, then Claudia, followed by Enrique, and a few others. In fact, we had to borrow chairs from nearby tables so that we could all fit. I introduced myself to everyone letting know that I was a graduate student and excited to learn along with them. I could see some of their eyes widen when I mentioned my doctoral program, and I promised that I would tell them more about it someday.

Each week, the same group of students came back and shared their enthusiasm for *The House on Mango Street* and other books that they had never heard of either. I was one step ahead of them, at least. At times, I stumbled over some of the Spanish dialogue in the texts, wishing I could roll my r's, but I could tell the students appreciated the effort. Periodically, they would ask me what I thought about a particular passage hoping that they got the analysis right, but I would volley back to them.

"Doesn't matter. What matters more is what <u>you</u> think, as long as you can back it up. Make sense?"

The crew nodded, eyes scanning the pages with a bit more certainty. I felt it, too. I opened the book, ready to lead.

I DON'T WANNA WAIT (PART ONEs)

In memory of DUSK ONE and Kate Karaguezian

"LT, you need to start watching again. Pacey is falling in love *with Joey.*"

It was Jim, my fellow cohort member in the English Department. Like me, he was from the East Coast—Philadelphia, specifically—but unlike me, Jim already earned a master's degree in Asian American Studies. He attended UPenn for undergrad, and we often joked about the bullet I dodged by not going there for graduate school as I had planned and dreamed of.

In addition to our East Coast roots, Jim and I bonded over our working-class backgrounds. One day, while taking a needed break from reading, I told him about the only time I had ever been to an overnight camp, the summer that the *E.T.* movie was released.

"Police Camp?" he practically spat out. "What in the world is Police Camp?! Did you want to become a cop??"

And it wasn't until that moment that I realized that this special opportunity, this camp that I both looked forward to and dreaded because I wasn't sure if I would know any of the other kids, was distinct. Like Toys For Tots, it was, in fact, a city-funded program for "at-risk" and "disadvantaged" youth with "financial need," I discovered when I did a Yahoo search later that night. Recognition slowly settled in as I recalled that most of the other campers were Black and how I did not know many of them well because they were not in my classes during the school year.

"Uck," I said back to him. "That's too bad."

I started watching "Dawson's Creek" during its second season when I needed to procrastinate for school. The good thing about taking classes during my first three years in my doctoral program was that they structured my day. Three or four days a week I had a destination, a purpose, and a reason to get out of the house no matter how annoying and boring those graduate seminars were. Without them, I had to fill my time and also make sure that I was making "good progress" on my own.

After completing my course requirements, I felt like I had my training wheels removed along with a forceful shove from behind to help me get to my destination faster—the Ph.D. The bike was wobbly, and I couldn't decide whether to keep pedaling or to thrust my legs out to the side to maintain balance. At this stage of the program, there were only self-imposed deadlines, and no one was making me do anything. I advanced or stalled at my own discretion. My dissertation advisors, the wonderfully supportive Valerie Smith and

Richard Yarborough, were busy helping other graduate students, teaching courses, and also furthering their own research agendas. No one was looking over my shoulder and checking in with me. I had to find ways to stay motivated as I worked towards my dissertation proposal.

Like any normal person, I hated the Dawson and Joey pairing on "Dawson's Creek," but I loved Pacey and Andie, the B story couple, especially Pacey, played by Joshua Jackson, who initially was a sidekick character. A funny thing happened along the way over the course of the show. Thanks in large part to Josh's charm, Pacey became more of a central figure, especially after the character revealed his crush on Joey, the former love interest of his best friend, Dawson. Joey Potter, played by 90s It Girl Katie Holmes, was a pill in my estimation, and Pacey Witter could do so much better.

After I gave birth to our son, Jabari, I took a break from the show and decided that I should focus on being a better television role model for him.

And school. I needed to focus on school, too. I had to justify why I could not definitely say when I would earn this Ph.D. or why Rob and I moved all the way to California just to end up broke.

Jim's words intrigued me though. I thought back to my first or second year in the program when Nick, who also was in our cohort, insisted that I watch "Friends," a newish comedy on NBC.

"No way," I protested. That show was waaaaay too white for me. And this was coming from someone who watched "Seinfeld" and "Mad About You" religiously and unironically.

"Watch it for Chandler," Nick said quite seriously. I did, and while I still thought "Friends" was white with a capital W, Chandler Bing indeed became my favorite character because of Matthew Perry's sharp, deadpan comedic delivery and because the character—and the actor—approached life with a certain lighthearted irreverence. I could relate.

Reluctantly, while putting complete faith in Jim's judgment, I decided to give "Dawson's" another shot tuning in late season three. Having once been in my own tortured teen love triangle back in high school, the entanglement between Pacey, Dawson, and annoying Joey seemed relatable.

Once Pacey and Jo sailed off into the sunset on a very modest sailboat headed south in the Atlantic Ocean, I was hooked. I spent the summer on messenger boards, reading fanfiction on websites powered by Tripod and speculating what would come next.

The analytical skills that I sharpened in my doctoral program were put to good use as I was able to quickly pick up on storylines and narrative arcs to better inform my predictions and make sense of the spoilers that were leaked online at websites like Television Without Pity, a pre-cursor to *The A.V. Club* and Twitter.

I Don't Wanna Wait (Part Ones)

I discovered that I had a lot in common with little Joey Potter besides being in love with Pacey Witter. She was more neurotic than me and worried about tests and grades more than I ever had, but I could relate to her desperate attempts to leave her small town and make her way to college by any means possible. The first in her working-class family to go to college, Jo was determined to get out of Capeside, start over, and see the world.

But what about the supportive high school boyfriend that she loved so much? Pacey, also from a blue-collar background, was tied to that very past that she was trying to escape. Could she bring him along? <u>Should</u> she bring him along? Would he hold her back? Or would he, the person who knew her best, who understood her roots, who was just as scrappy and determined as she was, be the thing that propelled her forward?

❊ ❊ ❊

When it became clear that I was going to attend UCLA for graduate school, Rob and I decided to drive the 3,000 plus miles from the apartment in Greenbelt, Maryland that we shared with my mother all the way to Connie's small apartment in South L.A. where we slept on her floor. We hitched a Budget rental, attached it to the back of our dusty Ford Escort, and drove for four days and three nights through several states all the while listening to a gigantic box of tapes that included Jodeci, Mary J. Blige, and Slick Rick. We ranked that road trip higher than our wedding, which had taken place two years prior.

My father, who had been in prison for most of my childhood, was back in Alexandria at this time. Through awkward stops and starts, we attempted to build a relationship toward the end of my time in high school. I even stopped by his apartment on my way to prom—in a $200 dress that Granddaddy had paid for.

I invited him to the wedding, but he never showed, and I pretended like I didn't care. Given all that he had done for me, including springing for that white Southern Belle gown back in high school, I figured that it made most sense to ask Granddaddy, who felt more like a benefactor than a father figure, to walk me down the aisle. It was a modest ceremony and reception, and it looked like those I had seen on TV. But I kept thinking that Rob and I should have just hosted a Spades tournament, watched the Fab Five play a basketball game, and called it a day.

The family drama was all behind us now. With thousands of highway miles before us each day, Rob and I were crazy in love, feeling like we were on the run, shouting the lyrics to Jodeci's "Stay" out of the window, while the cloudless sky hovered above.

🏀 🏀 🏀

To supplement my $14,000 school stipend, I tutored undergraduates as part of the campus AAP program, and the extra $6,000 or so that I earned teaching in the summer definitely helped with expenses. Meanwhile, Rob worked full-time selling car insurance and had yet to complete the degree that he started back at George Mason University in Virginia. After serving in the Persian Gulf War, he started working at a bank in Alexandria, and school slid down the list of priorities. Whenever he could, he took classes here and there at local community colleges in Maryland and now in California, but the credits weren't adding up to a degree or a credential.

It was challenging for me to spend my days at coffee shops in the West L.A., Mar Vista, and Hollywood neighborhoods while Rob woke up and left the house at the same time every day dressed in a shirt and tie and headed to the same three-story office building. Meanwhile, I, dressed in baggy jeans with a long button down thrown over a graphic tee, read books all day. At times, it seemed like our professional paths were diverging and that we were no longer headed in the same direction.

If I wasn't reading novels, then I was parked in front of a heavy Gateway desktop computer composing literary analyses and printing multiple essay drafts on our dot matrix printer. And if I wasn't doing either of those things, then I was in front of a computer writing messages to people all over the country, most of whom were 10 or more years younger than me, about whether or not Pacey should follow Joey to college.

People back home didn't know what I was doing in graduate school. Neither did I, really. For a long time, Rob's mom thought that I taught second grade.

To smooth things over and ease my guilt for leaving, I sent UCLA merch back home to Grandma and my other family members. The school had a recognizable name with an impressive pedigree of sports championships, and I knew that a fresh hoodie direct from Westwood would make a great conversation starter whenever Grandma made her way to the pharmacy and bumped into her friends. ("Oh, this thing? My granddaughter goes to UCLA.") For shorthand, my uncles and my cousins simply called me "Doc" (although I had not completed my Ph.D.) and told all of the neighbors and their friends that I was a college professor. I always had been, in their estimation.

"Babe," I said to Rob one day. "Why don't you just go back to school full-time?"

I took one quarter off after I gave birth to our son Jabari and returned right back to teaching and finishing up my coursework. It did help when I received a Ford Foundation Predoctoral Award, a prestigious fellowship for underrepresented graduate students, which covered UCLA tuition and fees for three years and also provided an annual $14,000 stipend for living expenses, replacing and not supplementing the one that I received from the school. I received periodic increases over the years from other sources, and the most I ever made was $17,000 for being a teaching assistant or research assistant. I remember feeling incredulous when I heard that the University of Southern

California paid $25,000 each year for graduate student fellowships.

With a young child, Rob and I needed to pay for full-time childcare so that I could get this Ph.D. over with and start making real money. But for the moment, we were broke.

I rationalized that things couldn't get much worse financially, so Rob might as well go back to school, too, so that he would qualify for higher paying jobs with an earned degree. It took some cajoling but Rob transferred to a local university, and we agreed that he should go full-time to help expedite things. He cut back his work hours, and we used student loans to supplement our income, most of which we used to pay for daycare.

At one point, our combined income and full-time student status qualified us for public assistance and for a period of time we used those government checks to cover formula, grape juice, and fresh vegetables (but not diapers). We never made quite enough money to last between pay periods, so we got in the habit of going to the payday loan building that was within walking distance of UCLA graduate housing where we lived. Rob received an advance on his paycheck so that we could pay for things that came up in the middle of the month, but then we had to pay a loan fee that reduced his earnings even more, which meant that we had to keep returning to the payday loan building on a regular basis because we always came up short. It felt like an endless cycle.

Here I was attempting to earn a doctorate and propel myself and my family forward but feeling like I was taking so many steps backwards. Mom made sure that Jabari had all of the books, Thomas the Tank Engines, and toy dinosaurs that a kid could ever want, but for the most part, Rob and I were toughing it out, and praying for the day when everything would pay off.

❖ ❖ ❖

Jim was one of several graduate students of color that I connected with, especially in the early years of my graduate program. In addition to Connie, I thought that Jim, along with students like Mike, Daphne, Tammy, and others, were incredibly and ridiculously smarter than me. I was stunned by their vocabulary and the seemingly easy way they seemed to recall literary theory.

With Connie coming to campus less regularly, after she finished her course requirements, I hung out with Kate, another classmate, and we watched a lot of bad TV together. While I was still taking graduate seminars, Kate was one of my best friends in the program. She grew up in Palo Alto, attended a high school right across from Stanford University, and also attended college there. I couldn't believe it when she told me that her mother had earned a doctorate and was "just" (in my estimation) a housewife. But Kate downplayed her mom's education and noted that by Palo Alto standards, her family was on the "lower side." She had been a scholarship kid in high school and college and winced whenever anyone referred to her as white.

"My dad is Armenian," she would say her lips forming a straight horizontal line.

During my first year in the department, when all I did was take classes and tutor on the side, I was not confident in my abilities and rarely spoke in class for fear that I might say something wrong and be exposed as a fraud. By my second and third year, things were different. Whereas before my face would burn hot if I didn't know something or was called on directly in class, by this time I had no problem asking my peers to explain a term to me.

"I'm sorry," I would say looking them directly in the eye. "I don't know what you mean. Can you clarify?"

In Professor Claire McEachern's graduate seminar on Shakespeare, I was one of only two students, and so the three of us—Claire, my classmate, and I—simply met in Claire's office for two and a half hours each week. I was living on the edge. Many weeks, I hadn't even read the plays and would just show up and see how much I could get away with. My trick was to make a comparison to something I had read.

"Hmm," I nodded thoughtfully with a water bottle in my hands. "Yes. The imagery in this passage reminds me of [insert name of something else entirely]."

Claire and my lone peer would light up and affirm that this was indeed a powerful connection that I made.

"Very smart," Claire would say, lean back in her chair, and then move on to something else.

It became a game to me. I learned that it really didn't matter what I was saying as much as how I said it. Say it with confidence and most of the time people believed you or at least didn't openly disagree with you. I noticed that my white male peers—in their faded jeans, graphic tees, and long-sleeved flannel—did the same.

But my cockiness didn't last. After coursework, the next step of our doctoral program was the successful completion of an oral qualifying exam, which we informally called the "Part Ones," during which we would demonstrate broad knowledge of three sub-fields in literature. Three faculty representatives from each of these fields would sit around a seminar table and ask general questions we might anticipate in a job interview for a faculty position, such as: how would we teach a literature course about the Civil War? Or what three texts would we use to teach an introductory course on modernism?

My three fields were 19th Century American, 20th Century American, and African American literature, and to prepare, I studied with a couple of elders in the department, including Jim and Connie, who had already passed the exam a year before. One weekend, a small group of us traipsed over to someone's apartment for a mock exam that I asked for. My stomach started to feel queasy, and I couldn't keep anything down. As we settled down in the living room, my body started shaking, and I felt like I needed to poop. Despite my attempts to suppress it, I couldn't stop my voice from wavering when I spoke. I was in my head, for sure, I didn't want to appear dumb, and I did not want to let down my peers who were like my superheroes.

Instead of sitting at a table for the mock exam, I crouched on the floor in the bathroom while Jim sat in the hallway outside of the door and lobbed questions my way. His voice was steady and reassuring from the other side.

"Just take a deep breath," he said. "Just keep going."

Tears streamed down my face the whole while I talked about Henry James and Ernest Hemingway, but I got through the mock, and I passed the real exam, as well, thanks to the unconditional support of my peers.

I never pretended that I loved taking classroom seminars, and after the Part Ones, I didn't pretend like I wanted to enroll in another class in order to expand my mind for learning's sake. In fact, immediately after I received my final graded paper from my last seminar, I took it out of my mailbox in the English department and dropped it straight in the recycling bin. I didn't even look at the grade or the comments.

❀ ❀ ❀

Besides Rob's steadiness and my graduate school colleagues' support, teaching kept me sane. After my first year in the doctoral program, I graduated from being an AAP tutor to leading my own weekly discussion sections in the English Department and eventually teaching entire seminars aimed at new first-year students and transfers. Dr. Chris Mott, a sensei who shepherded us through a seminar about teaching for new instructors, didn't pull any punches about what we might expect in the classroom.

"Students often try and take advantage of female instructors," he warned us. "especially if they are women of color, and particularly if they are of small stature."

Everyone in the seminar looked my way sending sympathy and premature condolences. *Oh, well.*

Dr. Mott raised these issues not to be cruel or snarky but as an acknowledgement that students typically treated female instructors differently than their male counterparts. In the teaching seminar we prepped for antagonism, and Dr. Mott assured us that he would have our backs and made sure that we knew about Title IX resources in the spirit of it is better to be safe and prepared than sorry.

I never encountered any discipline problems, though. In fact, teaching was a great outlet and a welcome distraction from coursework and ultimately deciding my dissertation topic, which loomed over me. I much preferred teaching non-majors and first year students. English majors, like some of my graduate school peers, seemed entitled and haughty—too eager to flex their knowledge about Edward Said and Stanley Fish. I wanted to be in the trenches with new students—both first-year students and transfers—and those taking writing classes as a dreaded requirement. I prided myself on reaching that population, helping students feel confident in their writing and finding their voice, as cliche as it sounded. I knew what it was like to be confused and frustrated and to play the game when I barely knew the rules.

For a period of time, my favorite class to teach was English A, which only was offered twice a year at the university: once during the summer and once during the fall. This non-credit bearing class was meant to provide a foundation to the handful of UCLA students who did not pass the Subject A writing placement exam that all California high school students took in the late spring, often during the same weekend as their prom. From English A, those students would go on to take another writing class before finally enrolling in English 3, first-year composition.

Many of these students in English A were class valedictorians and nearly all of them had attended a public high school. Most were first-generation to college or students of color. During the first week or so of class they would often arrive full of shame and doubt. Did they really earn their spot at UCLA often was the unspoken elephant in the room. In their minds, not passing the English A exam was just confirmation that they didn't belong even if they were the top student at their respective high school. I quickly realized that my job wasn't just to remind them of writing basics but to fill them with confidence and swagger before the fall quarter began.

I had a lot of flexibility in designing these courses as I nudged the students into what was considered "college writing," and I helped them build upon their critical thinking skills. Pop culture, including analyzing song lyrics, pinpointing which specific scene Michael Corleone becomes the godfather, or creating a grammatical superhero was just the way in.

Whenever possible, I incorporated basketball or sports into the curriculum, such as the time I had a group of students play a regular pickup game during class and then play according to the rules designated for women in the early 20th century. This meant that the players couldn't leave their designated areas on the court and had to adjust to making thoughtful passes in order to score and not just drive to the hoop anytime they wanted to.

"This sucks!" they yelled at me, especially the students who happened to play for either the school's men's or women's teams. But eventually, once they mastered the new rules, they found that they actually enjoyed this version of basketball.

"I feel like the game has slowed down, and I understand it better," said the novice players.

"Now I have to pick my spots and not waste time dribbling," said a rookie recruit on the men's team.

"Good," I said. "It's the same way with college writing. I know they are annoying at first, but you have to know the rules about commas and sentence fragments. Once you get those down, you can speed it up and make layups in your papers because you know the basics."

In other classes, not just English A, I would invite authors, actors, or other "real people" in the local area to class so that students could hear directly from these artists and creators. This is how I came to meet Nina Revoyr, author of one of my favorite novels, *The Necessary Hunger*, about a Japanese American female high school basketball player in Southern California. I did a Google search, came across her email address, and invited her to class.

I also invited former child actor Dante Basco to a screening that I hosted on campus to talk about his role in an indie movie, *Fakin Da Funk*, about a Chinese American boy (although Basco identifies as Filipino American) who is adopted by a Black family (Pam Grier played his adopted mother!). While living in Atlanta, the blended family is fully accepted by the local community. Problems arise when they move to Los Angeles, where racial and ethnic identity are more closely guarded and policed. I noted that Basco's character Julian is ridiculed and the butt of awful racial stereotyping about Asian men – until he proves he can ball on a public basketball court.

At the time, Dante was best known as Rufio from Steven Spielberg's interpretation of Peter Pan in the movie *Hook*. It would be another eight years before he would voice the iconic character Zuko for the animated television series, "Avatar: The Last Airbender."

I DON'T WANNA WAIT (PART TWOs)

There's no manual for choosing a dissertation topic and coming up with an area of study that I needed to stick with *for years* was even worse than figuring out what graduate programs to apply for. This "project," as it was referred to amongst the doctoral student community, would be my calling card, so I needed to pick a damn good one.

When I was only in my first or second year, I remember bumping into Mike, who was a few cohorts ahead of me, in the computer lab reserved for graduate students in our department. Once students completed coursework and passed the Part One exam, they seemed to disappear. We newbies mostly heard about them and felt lucky to see them at a department function or at someone's apartment during a weekend hang. These advanced students were known only by first names, and all the rest of us knew was that they were "writing." That's it. Mike, Daphne, Tracy, and Joni, who were at least three years ahead of me in the program, were "writing" and all seemed to sit on an academic Mount

Olympus and were untouchable. They came down the mountain only occasionally.

So, it was like a unicorn sighting when I saw Mike on this day. Being a rookie who was still learning the ropes and hopeful that my dissertation topic—whatever it turned out to be—would change hearts and minds and shake up the field and even ways of knowing, I asked Mike the unthinkable:

"What's your dissertation about?"

Everyone else in the room grew quiet and avoided eye contact squinting at their Macs to pretend like they couldn't hear this conversation. Mike laughed just like Alonzo in *Training Day* and paused.

"I wish I knew," he said.

I laughed along with him, but I was also confused and a little bit scared just like Jake in *Training Day*. He was writing a disser-tation. How could he not know what it was about? Mike was either a genius or a slacker, and I couldn't tell which.

A turning point came when I took a class with poet Harryette Mullen who was excited to discuss with us a sub-genre of African American literature that she referred to as "Affirmative Action Babies," that is, post-Civil Rights literature written by Black folks who were the beneficiaries of affirmative action—a new kind of middle class. These authors, including Trey Ellis and Andrea Lee, wrote about going to boarding school and to Stanford University. Some of the characters were obnoxious and completely unaware of their privileges. I couldn't relate to their plight, but I loved talking about contemporary literature, not just the classics like *Narrative of the Life of Frederick Douglass* or *The Souls of Black Folk*.

Around this time, although I don't recall if it was as a result of this particular class, I discovered Paul Beatty's debut novel, *The White Boy Shuffle*, and it seemed like the world stopped. The book was quirky and a little bit cheeky. The name of one of the characters, Nick Scoby, became my go to password on all of my devices because I thought it was so dope.

I connected with the protagonist, Gunnar, immediately. I related to his love for basketball, his geekiness, his reluctance to be a folk hero. Additionally, the book takes place in Los Angeles, my adopted home, and when Gunnar talked about going to high school in West L.A., I knew exactly what streets he was referring to.

Based on my upbringing, I already was inclined to notice basketball anywhere, like on TV shows and on TV commercials, but now the sport was popping up in places where it wasn't supposed to be, like in the work of John Edgar Wideman or in the movie *Finding Forrester*, and I wanted to know why and to think about *what does it mean*?

But was this a dissertation-worthy project? My colleagues were writing about "important" topics like modernism, post-modernism, and post-post modernism. Jim's dissertation focused on "urban triage"; Daphne was writing about "spectacular performances"; Mike's dissertation, whatever it was about, surely had to be important, too. There were so many big, vague words in their titles, some which seemed made up, to be honest.

Before taking Harryette's class, I made half-hearted attempts to mimic what I was seeing. At one point, I considered a project about the prevalence of pimps in Black culture and literature. I came very close to writing my entire dissertation about the oeuvre of Iceberg Slim whom I still argue is a vastly underrated thinker and storyteller. I also wanted to write about hip hop music, particularly the art and vision of rapper and mogul Jay-Z, but the English department didn't seem equipped to support that kind of project in the way of coursework or faculty specialty. In truth, I was waiting for permission to pursue my own interests.

And then there was Connie, once again pointing the way. She decided to write her dissertation about fitness literature, and it included no canonical writers. This gave me confidence to move forward. In addition to his affection for "Dawson's Creek," Jim was an avid "X Files" watcher. Mike was, too. Daphne wrote a lot about pop music, including Jeff Buckley. Although the English Department did not offer courses on pop culture at this time and only one person on my dissertation committee—Richard Yarborough—knew anything about basketball, the environment was supportive. No one challenged the topic's merit, and most faculty in the department—Claire McEachern and Helen Deutsch, an 18th century scholar, among them—were eager to see how I would approach the work. I moved forward with a project that explores contemporary African American literature by male writers and how basketball is used as a way to explore racial authenticity—or what it means to be Black.

At this stage of the program—after completing courses and passing my Part Ones—I drew support from three other friends in the department: Molly, Lars, and Andrew. Lars and I were in the same cohort; Molly and Andrew were one year behind us. It helped that all of us focused on modern American Literature. We studied together, and we met at each other's apartments in West L.A. and exchanged ideas about our nascent dissertation projects in preparation for the dissertation defense, otherwise known as Part Twos. With this group, I was not afraid to sound stupid as I pitched alliterative project titles ("Hoops, Hype, and Homies" or "Dribble, Dunk, Disrupt") even though I had yet to write a single word; or I wondered if I could invite Jay-Z to be my outside reader. We were trying out ideas to see what stuck and landed.

We also shared our aspirations for becoming full-time faculty members somewhere, especially at teaching institutions or small private colleges where we felt like we could make real impacts with students. None of us had ambitions to teach in a research institution like UCLA, and all four of us wanted to work directly with undergraduate students. Working at a research institution meant getting farther away from undergrads.

Additionally, I was deadset on returning back East to be closer to family. I imagined myself at a place like Simmons University in Boston or Trinity College in Washington, D.C. where Mom had eventually earned her bachelor's degree at age 44.

❀ ❀ ❀

For a period of time, I paused teaching, ostensibly so that I could focus on my dissertation. While I loved working directly with students, it really was time consuming, and it was easy and more fulfilling to help new students create strong thesis statements than it was for me to sit my ass down and write. I picked up a job as a research assistant with the Program in African American Studies and the Cultural Studies in the African Diaspora Project located in Haines Hall where I worked on research projects for my dissertation co-chair Valerie Smith, professor Marcyliena Morgan, and even alumnus and basketball Hall of Famer, Kareem Abdul-Jabbar.

While there, I met Tarek, a pale-skinned and lanky undergraduate sociology major, who was an office assistant. From our casual conversations I learned that Tarek, who preferred to be called "Dusk," was a fellow hip hop head and a local dee jay. At first, my instinct was to code him as Black and to put him in a box because of his passion for the culture. But I would come to learn that he was of proud Middle Eastern heritage. We became inseparable.

Sometime in 1998, while we chatted about the latest albums from Jay-Z, Juvenile, and Blackstar, and after Dusk surely would've schooled me on some obscure graffiti artist that I never heard of, we came up with an idea.

"You know what? We should organize a hip-hop conference," Dusk said.

Back in 1991, while I was still a student there, Howard University hosted the first ever national hip hop conference held at a college or university. And there hadn't been another since. So much about the culture and the industry had changed since then, and we knew it was time. Hip hop was expanding into a number of areas besides music, and artists—like Jay-Z—were making imprints on fashion and other industries.

I nodded and gave Dusk a high five across our desks.

Dreaming big, we wanted "POWER MOVES" to promote meaningful dialogue between critical theorists, ethnomusicologists, community activists, performers, undergraduate and graduate students, and academics, among others.

"We understand that power does not stand still; in fact, power *moves* on a regular basis," we declared in our proposal to the African American Studies Center that we approached for funding. Dusk was adamant that we highlight all aspects of the culture, i.e., dance, music, art, and DJing. I was interested in how hip hop moved outside of music and how it impacted films, sports, and fashion. We wanted to balance well-known performers with those that were not in the mainstream but equally impactful. And we made sure that women were a major part of every panel.

We had some input from advisors Professor Smith and Professor Morgan, but primarily we were left to ourselves. Dusk and I recruited other graduate and undergraduate students to serve on the planning committee. Our small but mighty crew sent eager letters to the likes of Queen Latifah, along with Jay-Z and the newish Roc-A-Fella Records. We reached out to Skechers, an up-and-coming company based out of Manhattan Beach, California located south of us on the 405 freeway. Not only was Skechers our first official sponsor—I screamed in the office while Dusk popped and locked to celebrate— they sent us a box of sneakers to give away.

In the end, we had a dream event in mid-May 1999. Hip hop spokesperson Fab 5 Freddy was our keynote speaker. Our panelists included choreographer Big Lez; Davey D of KMEL radio in San Francisco; Boots Riley from The Coup; Karen Good, my former Howard University classmate who was now writing for *honey* and *Vibe* magazines; and many more hip-hop contributors. We screened *Krush Groove* at the UCLA James Bridges Theater and hosted a conversation with Ralph Farquhar, the screenwriter. We hosted a pre-party at Valentino's Lounge on Wilshire Boulevard and a closing ceremony at KAOS Network in Leimert Park.

Writing a dissertation was a drag—equal parts isolating and self-serving—but I felt motivated and purposeful while working with Dusk and putting the conference together. I curated and moderated a panel on hip hop films—not just those directly about the culture, but those *influenced by* the culture—including actor Tyrin Turner (*Menace II Society*); S. Craig Watkins, then an assistant professor from UT Austin; filmmaker and graffiti writer Mare 139; and recording artist and actor, Ice-T.

Being an eager and overconfident graduate student, as moderator, I asked Tyrin a ridiculously dense question about subjectivity and postmodernism that was more of a statement and a way for me to show off what I had learned in a Kierkegaard seminar. He just said, "Huh?" and looked at me sideways. I was embarrassed for him and for myself.

Ice-T easily was the biggest draw to the conference. I approached him at the end of the panel to show my appreciation.

"Thanks for being here!" I said, my hand extended.

Before he gripped it, T took a step back. "Whoa. What is this?" He looked me over.

Confused, I glanced down at the cherry red jersey that I was wearing with "Sixers" emblazoned across the chest. Ice-T also wore a red jersey, an iconic one featuring number 23. Michael Jordan of the Chicago Bulls had retired for the second time only a few months prior in January 1999. It was clear that Ice-T was paying his respects to the GOAT.

"Iverson," I replied sticking my chin out a little.

Ice-T tsked at me and then began to address the onlookers who were standing nearby.

"See? This is what I'm talking about," he said in that trademark growly voice. Then he shook his head. "These young bucks out here, coming into the league, got their own jerseys and everything."

He puffed out his chest in mock indignation, making a show and expanding the Bulls name.

Sure, MJ was regarded as one of the best to ever play the game, but Allen Iverson was special. At a mere 6 feet tall—short for NBA standards—he was a Virginia native and also a Georgetown alumnus, which is when I started following his career. He had only been in the league for three years and had been named Rookie of the Year in 1997. With his cornrows, baggy jeans, multiple chains of jewelry, and bad boy attitude, Iverson embodied a hip-hop aesthetic, and I thought it was only right to honor him at this conference.

I could tell that Ice-T was unimpressed with Iverson's resume which was a little thin at the time. T and Jordan represented the OGs. Iverson and I were in a younger, scrappy generation who still needed to earn our stripes. Within two years, Iverson would be named the league's Most Valuable Player and would lead his team to the NBA finals in an unlikely run, ultimately succumbing to the Los Angeles Lakers who were the defending champions. We couldn't see that far in the future, of course, but I knew that Iverson was a star in the making. He even shared a birthday with Prince.

I came in close for a picture with Ice-T, puffed out my own chest, and smiled.

"Just you wait," I told him. "You'll see."

DUCK MOUTH

(This is not a fairytale.)

My grandfather, known as "Pops" to some, "Granddaddy" to me, and "Mr. Wise" or "That Man" to Mom, was not my mother's biological father. A Navy veteran and a hot catch in their small town, like a Negro Prince Charming he married my grandmother when she already had four children of her own and a bad reputation because she had multiple baby daddies. The newly married couple, along with my mother, who was no more than seven years old, departed North Carolina and relocated to Northern Virginia where Grandma already had relatives.

For a number of years, they lived in Alexandria housing projects before buying their own home–an idyllic three story rowhouse with a yard–on Mount Vernon Avenue becoming only the second Black family in the neighborhood. For a time, Grandma worked a variety of jobs including as a checker at JC Penneys; Granddaddy had a steady job carrying mail.

My big cousin Lenita, who grew up in a one-story home in the small town of Williamston, North Carolina, once told me that as a child she was in awe of my grandparents' house that had three bedrooms on the very top floor, and a separate dining room, kitchen, and living room. She had never seen a basement before and remembers playing baseball down there while it was being built up. There was so much space and possibility.

Not long after they moved to that house, Mom, who was around 14 years old at the time, was sitting on the front porch with a friend when she heard what had now become a familiar noise from inside.

Banging.

Yelling.

The sound of flesh crashing into flesh.

She headed down to the basement and was faced with my grandfather's back. Before her was my grandmother.

"Don't you put your hands on my mother," Mom said through gritted teeth.

He never turned around, just hit Grandma again.

Her mind made up, Mom went upstairs to the kitchen and returned with a knife. My grandfather struck my grandmother again. Mom shoved the knife in his back, my grandmother screamed, and Mom went back up the stairs, called the ambulance and, with her back to the house and facing the train tracks across the street, waited on the porch for the authorities to arrive.

🏀 🏀 🏀

I was the first baby and grandchild to live in the house and was regularly doted on. With my hair in two pigtails or braided into neat cornrows, and my eyes large and clear like a Muppet, I was cute, smart, and precocious. Most people called me "Tee" or "T-Bone" or sometimes a variation on my name: "Lil' Tonya." Granddaddy insisted on calling me "Duck Mouth." He said it was because of my wide grin and my thin lips that slightly curled when I smiled. Maybe he thought the name was cute, but I shuddered every time he said it. I hated the way it drew attention to something I couldn't change, as if my features were somehow a joke like Daffy Duck.

The name felt more like a badge of shame than honor. It was like he and I were the only two members of a club that I wanted no part of, a flimsy straw house built on teasing and discomfort. I wanted my house to be brick-solid, built on names like "Tee" that made me feel strong and loved.

Although I was chided for talking too much and reading all of the time, Granddaddy made sure that I had access to a complete set of eggshell white World Book Encyclopedias that he started buying before I was born. Each month, over two years' time, a new book would arrive in the mail. The encyclopedias were never updated and the information that I had was frozen in 1974, but at least I had the entire alphabet. Granddaddy beamed with pride whenever he saw me at the dining room table browsing through a book, pulling the slick, sticky pages apart.

Mom said it was overcompensation: Granddaddy treated me better than he treated his step children (Mom, my aunt Roberta, and my uncles Ronnie and Rudy) or even his own biological son, my uncle Dale, the youngest of the five. Eventually, there would be a revolving door of grandchildren whose parents—my uncles—would drop off while they served time, or kicked drug habits, or got their lives together.

I became the cousin that my other cousins—mostly boys—were compared to.

The first time that I made the honor roll at G.W. Junior High, Granddaddy placed a bumper sticker ("I Have an Honor Roll Student") on the back of his blue Ford pick up.

"What?" Grandma clucked her tongue. "I didn't think he would ever put *anything* on that funky old truck."

She slammed a frying pan on the stove.

"She's the smart one," Granddaddy would announce to no one in particular. "The rest of those motherfuckers ain't worth shit."

Seven years my junior, Little Ronnie was on the brunt end and witnessed too much. He was only a toddler when his mother walked out leaving him and my uncle behind. Big Ronnie departed shortly thereafter, and Little Ronnie remained with my grandparents moving into the small bedroom at the end of the hallway that I used to occupy.

At least my mother came back for me. After Mom joined the Army and settled in, I was able to live with her in Texas and South Carolina.

But Little Ronnie stayed in the house on Mount Vernon Avenue, and he heard, and he saw.

I never saw Granddaddy hit Grandma. But I watched him stumble down the street and stagger into the house. I detected the pungent smell of cheap beer that made my stomach turn and made me forever hate the taste. I heard about the time Mom and her siblings—mere teenagers—jumped Granddaddy down in the projects when they got tired of him beating their mother. The threat of violence was always in the air in that house, existing just beneath the surface, seeped into the curtains and into the rugs, passed down from decades.

Being smart shielded me, as I was never on the receiving end of Granddaddy's sarcasm, scorn, wrath, or his fists. I felt like a survivor who stepped outside after a gusty tornado to find all of the houses around me leveled, while mine remained standing. Were my materials so different than everyone else's? Was Ronnie's house made of straw? Was mine made of brick?

Or was I just lucky?

❂ ❂ ❂

Once upon a time, I was in the basement of my grandparents' house, most likely listening to the radio or doing homework when I heard the familiar patter of Little Ronnie's footsteps racing down the creaky steps.

I looked up.

"What's wrong?"

His face was turning from pink to red.

"He hit her," Ronnie said, and then he started crying.

I was in high school at the time, which means that Little Ronnie would have been no more than 10 years old. From the time he started living with my grandparents and me on Mount Vernon Avenue when he was a baby, it was my job to watch over him. This was true when I changed his diapers and when I taught him how to read. It was true even when Mom and I later moved to South Carolina, and I made us fried baloney sandwiches and baked cakes using Quaker Instant Oatmeal when we were left alone during the summer he spent with us. And it was true in this moment.

A sharp pain shot through my chest.

He hit her?

My thoughts raced wildly.

While I was in the house?

I had only heard stories about this.

The audacity, I thought. I could not believe that Granddaddy would hit Grandma while I was there. My presence alone should have given him pause, as well as protected her and Little Ronnie.

I stormed up the wooden basement steps and the sound echoed like a drum beat throughout the rowhouse. The steps were uneven, worn down by years of restless feet—mine, Little Ronnie's, and everyone else's who'd come and gone through the house. I paused only to grab a rusty paring knife from the kitchen. It felt heavier than it should have, its blade speckled with dark stains I didn't want to think about, holding secrets I wasn't even aware of. I had no idea what I would do with it but holding it made me feel less small, less powerless.

Weapon in hand, I paused on the narrow stairwell leading to the top floor. The air was thick and stale, carrying the faint smell of menthol cigarettes and something fried from earlier in the day.

Grandma was in her bedroom with the door closed. There was no light under the doorway and no sound from her TV as though to deter any unwarranted visitors who dared knock on her door. From my place on the creaky stairs, I could see that Pop's room, a few doors down the hallway, also was shrouded in darkness. The bedroom door was open, and I could barely make out the shape of him sitting on the edge of the bed. The only light came from the dim orange glow of his cigarette as he inhaled, the ember flaring briefly like a warning, each of us waiting for the other to make the first move.

I felt dizzy like I was outside of myself watching this unfold. The knife in my hand was the only thing anchoring me, its cold handle pressing into my sweaty palm. My heart pounded so loud I was sure he could hear it, but he held still and exhaled deeply.

I sucked in a shaky breath, the words rising up from somewhere deep inside me.

"If you ever touch her again, I'll kill you," I whispered, the sound barely louder than a hiss. Then I turned, the knife still clenched in my hand as I descended the stairs and walked out of the house into the night.

※ ※ ※

As Mom had encouraged me to do, I set out in the world leaving Alexandria behind to seek my fortune in Los Angeles for graduate school. When I was pregnant with our son, Rob and I moved to UCLA graduate school housing, "premier community living," in West Los Angeles on the second floor of a sturdy, stucco covered brand new apartment building. The walls were thick and unyielding; the plumbing worked without complaint. Even the floors felt solid beneath my feet, although Rob and I still treaded softly so as not to disturb the neighbors below.

At night, I slept soundly, lulled by the faint hum of traffic from the 405 freeway instead of Amtrak train whistles. During the day, sunlight streamed through the windows. Seven miles from the Santa Monica beach, the salty air carried a promise of calm.

Now long past my Part Ones and Part Twos, the last hurdle to clear was my dissertation, which focused on the prevalence of basketball in contemporary narratives written by Black men. I also included memoirs written by NBA players like Michael Jordan, highlighting the moments when he asserted just how damn smart he was despite what the mainstream media said about him as an author or team owner.

When Jabari became a toddler, I would wake up between 5:00 and 6:00 a.m. to avoid distractions before he rose for the day and requested a juice box or Chicken Dinos. But many times, I would just stare at the computer screen. I didn't know what to write or how to even go about completing a dissertation.

You've written your whole life. I would tell myself. *Why is this so hard?*

I spent hours playing Yahoo Spades and chatting with my virtual friends, "dirtyoldlady" and "WitterWoman," on "Dawson's Creek" messenger boards.

Sometimes my mind would wander 3,000 miles east to Mount Vernon Avenue. I thought of Grandma and Little Ronnie still back there in the house. Ronnie had gone away to Virginia State University and—like a boomerang—returned after one semester. And even when he eventually moved out for good, he was never too far away, living for a long period of time in a rowhouse just across the street from our grandparents.

Looking for a distraction, I did a Google search, typing in random words like "home improvement" and "Alexandria" and stumbled across a city program for low-income residents. It offered to make repairs and would even provide brand new appliances, like a washer and dryer. There would be no monthly payments and no interest would accrue. Best of all, the loan was not due *for 99 years*. I called the office to verify that this was not a scam. All we needed was my grandfather's tax information.

Thoughts of my dissertation shoved aside, I called Grandma and explained the program as best as I could, breaking it down to its simplest elements: we can get the house fixed up with no upfront costs.

At quick glance the house seemed fine. But if you looked closely from the outside, you could see the paint peeling on the steps, the pipes that were dented. The kitchen was outdated, and the basement had become a dumping ground for old clothes and discarded appliances. Only the truly desperate used the bathroom in the back. Most of the time we just held our pee.

Grandma was onboard. Granddaddy was not.

"No," he huffed. "I don't care what it is. I'm not giving my taxes to those motherfuckers. Not over my dead body."

My rage, long simmered over decades, suddenly reached a boiling point, replacing the guilt I felt for leaving.

"You are so selfish!" I yelled into the phone, my body trembling and my temperature rising. "You don't care about anybody but yourself. Why can't you do *one thing* for Grandma for once? Do you just want the house to fall apart? Is that it? I can't stand you!"

Thoughts of dreams deferred and promises not kept swirled in my mind.

I had never spoken so sharply to him. Once again, I was on one side, he was on the other, and neither of us budged. A door slammed shut between us that day.

❄ ❄ ❄

Six years after I completed my doctorate, Granddaddy dropped to the floor in his bedroom and took his last breath in the house on Mount Vernon Avenue. The official diagnosis was lung disease. Most likely he had liver problems, too, after decades of drinking and given that the white of his eyes had turned yellow.

The house was almost unlivable at that point and on the brink of being condemned. In the bedroom where Granddaddy slept and died, all four walls were covered in a yellow film from nicotine stains. There were roaches throughout the house, especially in the kitchen and the basement, that most people had just come to accept and to ignore. All of the basement windows had been replaced with trash bags and at night, rodents would chew through them and scurry inside, making the house their home.

Thanks to military benefits from his short-lived active-duty stint in the Marines, Rob and I had recently purchased our own three bedroom corner home in South Los Angeles near the Crenshaw District, only a few miles from Connie's old apartment on Slauson Boulevard.

I went to my five-drawer file cabinet in my home office. I milled past the aborted dissertation projects on Jay-Z and music moguls and pimps and hos in Black culture that I half-heartedly attempted and moved my fingers beyond my dissertation chapters, each revision printed on different color printer paper. There, lurking in the back, was a red folder that contained only one item, a modest two-sided brochure for the Alexandria Home Rehabilitation Loan Program preserved as though it had been archived. I held it, feeling the weight of both my new house and the one I left behind.

Like I had done so many times over the years, I completed the form, mailed the application to Grandma, and told her where to sign.

LEGACY

an epilogue

When I attended Lonnie B. Nelson Elementary School for third grade, half of fourth grade, and then fifth grade, I had a singular goal: to beat everyone in a footrace.

And I trained for this accomplishment everywhere I could, just like Rocky Balboa. I ran wind sprints right in the middle of the street in my Charleswood neighborhood. Some days I pretended that I was at the Olympics with the gold medal on the line, and I crossed an imaginary finish line with arms in the air just like Wilma Rudolph.

I especially wanted to beat any boy.

"Race you to the red car!" I would yell at my neighbors, Spanky and Bay-Bay, and I would take off like a shot leaving them in the dust and struggling to keep up.

I also wanted to be the fastest girl on eight wheels, and I zoomed around in white boot roller skates both on the rocky asphalt in front of my house but also on Saturday afternoons at Foxcroft skating rink. I rolled my eyes and played Space Invaders and Galaga during the slow, boring couples skate; my turn to shine was a speed contest called Shoot The Duck where I zipped in and around the other skaters and was determined to be the youngest person in the rink left upright on wheels.

But mainly, I wanted to sprint on two legs far ahead of everyone even though it meant that the only thing in front of me was my own gray shadow.

❀ ❀ ❀

Buzz spread throughout the fifth-grade classes when we learned that there was going to be a major art project at the school.

A mural painting, our teacher explained, is like a giant picture painted on a wall.

She said, "Imagine if you took a piece of paper and drew a beautiful picture, but instead of using paper, you used a big wall."

Our eyes grew wide at the thought but also at the audacity of painting right on the wall, something we ordinarily would get in trouble for. We learned that artists create mural paintings to make places look pretty, to tell a story, or to share important messages with everyone who sees it. A mural is like a huge piece of art for everyone to enjoy in the public, not hidden in a museum or somebody's house. There were murals all over Washington, D.C.

In this case, our mural was meant to make our school look as beautiful on the inside as it was on the outside. And best of all, each of us was going to contribute to it.

For the next few weeks, instead of crowding into the art room, we spent class time working on the mural, which would be located a few yards away from the main office near the front of the school. Anyone who entered from the front doors would be able to see it.

At first, it was a boring outline, and we were not impressed. "That's it?"

It didn't look like any painting we had ever seen before. The design was outlined on the wall, nothing was colored in, and we couldn't tell what the picture was supposed to be in the end. For now, it was merely black tape on faded yellow walls.

"Why can't we just paint it all at once?" we whined to our teacher when the mural wasn't instantly completed in just one day.

Even worse, we had to use small brushes and paint with small strokes. It was taking so long, and our excitement started to dim. Some of us were ready to go back to the art room and start making masks out of paper plates, construction paper, and fuzzy pipe cleaners.

We had to stay in our assigned areas and work with the same color palette for weeks, which tested our ten-year-old patience. Our teacher assured us that everyone would be able to see our work when it was done, and we regarded her skeptically in return.

"This is boring," someone muttered under their breath.

But just as our teacher promised, over a few weeks' time, the pieces started to come together. My station wasn't near my best pals Gloria or Thomasina, but I didn't mind this time because I was so focused on my own section. Occasionally, I would check out what they were doing, and we would wave to one another from across the hall. I was sure to guard my area and got annoyed if another student painted too closely to it.

To this day, I do not recall what I painted, and I have no memory of the final mural—I think it was simply images of different kids. I do know that the paint I used was the color of silly putty, and that I had to wear a smock so that I would not get any of it on my clothes.

And I knew that whenever Mom came to the school, I could take her by the hand, walk her over to the wall, and point.

"There."

In the grand scheme of things, my section was small. It was easy to miss when you walked by on your way in or out of the building, but whenever we lined up to enter the cafeteria for lunch, I knew exactly the spot that I painted, and I would run my fingers over it along the concrete wall. [I knew this hallway well.]

I had several highs and lows while attending Lonnie B. I had been at the school for two and a half years starting in the third grade when Mrs. Zajkowski told me that I was smart and going to college some day. One year, I beat up a white classmate, Stacey Levine, after he called me a "nigger." I cried after I punched him in the face because Stacey was Jewish, and I thought he and I had an unspoken alliance because we were different than the other kids. Worse than the name calling, I felt betrayed.

In fourth or fifth grade, I was taunted and terrorized for months by a group of Black boys who spent their days coming up with ways to cop a feel on my backside, sometimes trapping me in the classroom after the teacher left. But I also learned my times tables, and I memorized all 50 states plus their capitals while I attended this school. One time, from the back of the classroom, emboldened by a popular song on the radio, I told a math teacher to "leave us kids alone!" when she got too snippy with a classmate. She couldn't believe that I, the only Black girl in advanced classes and who never spoke up, dared to challenge her authority.

After culminating from Lonnie B. Nelson, I would go on to enroll in six more schools before graduating from high school, attend three different universities, and live in multiple temporary residences in North Carolina, Virginia, Maryland, and Washington, D.C. But I didn't know that yet. What I knew at this time is that each day that I returned to this school, where I was the fastest girl in the whole fifth grade, I was leaving my mark. My legacy wasn't just in the mural we painted or the races I won on the playground; it was in the small moments that made me unforgettable, even after I was gone.

ACKNOWLEDGMENTS

"Anything is possible."
—KG

Honestly, I was mostly minding my business when Erica Alfaro, author of *Harvesting Dreams*, said to me during an Instagram Live that I really should tell the story that I needed when I was a student. Those words unpacked their bags in my mind, stayed with me, and made themselves at home putting their feet on the furniture and taking over my Netflix account. But here's that story, which means that I have a number of people to thank, including, of course, Erica.

To Gloria Rease a.k.a. Mom Dukes: Thank you for being my biggest fan. This book literally, and I mean *literally*, would not be possible without you.

Thank you, Rob, for always encouraging me to be me. *Strangé*!

Jabari and Zoe, I hope to be as cool as you are someday. I am so proud to be your mom. I'll stop here so that I don't say anything corny.

In the beginning and in the end was Genesis, my fearless editor and thought partner, who helped me shape all of these words into a project that I am truly proud of. You didn't just edit a book—you held space for a dream. #firstgenforever

Thanks to the Squad, the badass group of women who helped bring *Smart Girl* to life: Heather Adams, Anna Alves, Alejandra Campoverdi, Mel DeVivar, Xion Nelson, Samantha Pinto, and Irena Smith. Thank you for always being in my corner.

To my extended family: there are too many of you to name but thank you all for the support despite the miles apart. But special thanks to Unc, Jerry, LaShune, Lenita, Ronnie, and William for letting me share a little of your powerful stories with the world. I mean it when I say, *you need to write your own books*. Just sayin'.

Dani, Kim, and Megan: I only want to see you underneath the purple rain. Thank you for being the best ride or dies a girl could have.

To Angie, my forever captain, and Lalania, my BFF: I have so much gratitude for you taking the time to walk down memory lane with me and reminding me of the power of sisterhood.

Dusk and Kate, you departed this world too soon. I miss you dearly.

Tracy Buenavista, I have you to blame. Love you, girl, forever and always.

To the teachers, coaches, librarians, office managers, and custodians who saw something in a sleepy-eyed girl with impeccable shoes and her nose stuck in a book: thank you. You gave me a chance to dream bigger.

And to all of the smart girls out there reading this: You got next.

ABOUT THE AUTHOR

As a first-generation college graduate and thought leader in higher education, La'Tonya "LT" Rease Miles, Ph.D. has been instrumental in establishing successful programs for first-gen students at both UCLA and Loyola Marymount University. In her many leadership roles, including as co-founder of My Tribe Media and a co-founder of The Black First-Gen Collective, she advises institutions on first-gen student experiences. She regularly champions initiatives for non-traditional adult learners and contributes to scholarly discourse on first-gen experiences in popular culture. LT's influence extends to the digital sphere where she has co-founded several online communities, including a national Facebook group that empowers first-generation students.

After transferring from the University of NC at Chapel Hill and Howard University, La'Tonya earned a B.A. in English Literature from the University of Maryland at College Park and a Ph.D. in American Literature from UCLA.

www.ingramcontent.com/pod-product-compliance
Ingram Content Group UK Ltd.
Pitfield, Milton Keynes, MK11 3LW, UK
UKHW050203190225
455204UK00017B/148